"*Let the reader beware!* Dan Betzer reveals the Great Commission as the Great Commandment and catalogues the blessings found in obeying it, both for individuals and congregations. If you fear either conviction or inspiration, read something else!"

—**John Ashcroft, former Missouri governor, former Missouri senator, former attorney general of the United States**

"Dan Betzer is one of the greatest teachers and orators of our time. This book will open your heart to the true blessings of a thriving church through missions. And through missions the gospel will be sent to the ends of the earth!"

—**Dwight Evans, Boston Red Sox right-fielder 1972–1990**

"Every pastor should read this book. Period. Of course, I hope that all believers read it; but I'm especially concerned that pastors understand how this book will set their hearts on fire to reach the world for Jesus. No one I know has a greater passion for fulfilling the Great Commission than Dan Betzer. As a pastor and denominational leader, he has led his own church and multiplied others to increase their vision, passion, and support for the greatest cause ever—to do the greatest evangelism the world has ever seen."

—**Dr. George O. Wood, general superintendent, The General Council of the Assemblies of God**

"This book should be required reading for all pastors. With great clarity and personal insight, Dan Betzer simultaneously encourages and challenges us to boldly follow the Great Commission and become 'missions-minded.' This book will change your church forever."

—**Gail Ross, author and producer/host of *Testimonies of Triumph***

"In 1998, we started our church. The same year someone gave us an old cassette tape of a sermon by a man named Dan Betzer entitled, *"Why Some Churches Are Blessed."* We already had a heart for missions and believed in the power of faith and giving, but this message revolutionized our thinking on giving to missions. It changed our church forever! Sharing Dan's message has become an annual service that our congregation loves. Over the last sixteen years, our church has had the privilege of giving millions to missions. We attribute that largely to the message in this book. Read it for your sake, and for the sake of your church."

—**Mark and Janet Brazee, pastors of World Outreach Church, Tulsa, Oklahoma**

"I know of no one who embodies the message of global missions more than Dan Betzer. He is personal, passionate, and persuasive. The kingdom of God would be greatly expanded if *Why Some Churches Are Blessed* could become required reading in every church."

—**Alton Garrison, assistant general superintendent, The General Council of the Assemblies of God**

"In my twenty-five years at First Assembly of God in Fort Myers, Florida, I have seen the principles laid out in this book become the driving force of our amazing congregation. Dan Betzer has challenged us to believe that we *can* and *must* reach the world with the Great Commission. It isn't an option. Because of our uncompromising commitment to these principles, we have seen the impossible become reality. If you want to see your church go beyond the ordinary, read this book!"

—**David Thomas, associate pastor, First Assembly of God, Fort Myers, Florida**

"I came to know Dan Betzer in the early 1970's. My life has never been the same. I was a young youth pastor with a limited Pentecostal Assemblies of God background. I saw demonstrated in Dan's life a passion for the lost people of this world that ignited fire in my soul. He has modeled this passion for the lost throughout his ministry. When I think of missions and a symbiotic relationship between word and deed my mind defaults to Dan. Without question, he reflects and mirrors the heart of God for missions."

—**Gregory M. Mundis, DMin, executive director, The Assemblies of God World Missions**

"Why some churches seem to be blessed more than others may be a question you have asked and are still wondering about. Dan Betzer believes the answer is *giving to missions*! And he has convincing evidence to back it up. While giving over thirty-five million dollars to missions at home and abroad, the church he pastors has grown exponentially in every area of ministry, including about 7,000 regular attendees. This book tells an amazing story that every follower of Jesus Christ should read!"

—Dave Weston, former senior adult ministries director for
The General Council of the Assemblies of God

"Dan Betzer gets it. He gets what so many don't—that you can't build a great church without missions. Some pastors think they need to build buildings, polish presentations, and 'grow' their church before missions can matter to them. Missions matters to God . . . so missions has to matter to us. Pastors who have ignored the Great Commission will find conviction and challenge in Betzer's words. Pastors who have obeyed Christ's clarion call to reach the lost around the world will find encouragement and blessing. Either way, every pastor—and every layperson—should read this book!"

—David M. Wigington, lead pastor, Cornerstone Christian Fellowship,
Bloomington, Indiana

"Dan Betzer lives and breathes missions. It consumes him . . . and as a result, hundreds of missionaries are able to fulfill their calls; thousands have been born again; and the church of First Assembly is incredibly blessed! The principles that have propelled First Assembly to be an extraordinary missions-engaged church are transferable, and they are clearly articulated in this book! I dare you to implement some of these missional concepts!"

—Doug Clay, general treasurer, The General Council of the Assemblies of God

"There are few people who have had a more profound impact on my understanding of how to mobilize the church to reach the nations than Dan Betzer. In his book *Why Some Churches Are Blessed*, he shares some valuable insights from decades of effective ministry."

—John Lindell, lead pastor, James River Assembly, Ozark, Missouri

"This is a story that needs telling. Dan Betzer is not only one of the finest communicators of our time, but his passion for the global reach of Christ's church is both inspiring and strategic. The very heart of God comes through loud and clear."

—James Bradford, general secretary, The General
Council of the Assemblies of God

"Dan Betzer emphasizes that when you put missions as a priority, it positively impacts every area of church ministry and finance. This book must be a priority for every pastor."

—Clarence W. St. John, superintendent, Minnesota District Council, Minneapolis, Minnesota

"Dan Betzer takes the Word of God literally when it says "all" and "everyone." He has a contagious passion to see people introduced to Jesus and to give them the opportunity to become effective disciples. He was *missional* before it was trendy! His passion to see the church function as *the church* is nothing short of awe-inspiring. His congregation, staff, community, and friends have caught his vision. If you're in the boat with Dan Betzer, you'll want to get out of the boat and walk on the water with him!"

—George Westlake III, lead pastor, Sheffield Family Life Center; assistant superintendent, Southern Missouri District of The Assemblies of God, Kansas City, Missouri

WHY SOME CHURCHES ARE

BLESSED

PUTTING FAITH AND OBEDIENCE INTO ACTION

DAN BETZER

Published by Gospel Publishing House
1445 N. Boonville Ave.
Springfield, Missouri 65802
www.gospelpublishing.com

Cover design by Sheepish Design (www.sheepishdesign.org)
Interior design by Tom Shumaker

Produced with the assistance of Livingstone, the Publishing Services Division of Barton-Veerman Company (www.livingstonecorp.com). Project staff includes: Bruce Barton, Ashley Taylor, and Tom Shumaker.

ISBN: 978-1-60731-407-3

Printed in the United States of America

19 18 17 16 15 • 2 3 4 5

This book is dedicated
to the memory of the late
Dr. Oswald J. Smith,
legendary pastor of the
People's Church in Toronto, Canada.

He changed my life.

CONTENTS

FOREWORD

I RECENTLY ATTENDED SERVICES AT JAMES RIVER CHURCH IN SPRINGFIELD, MISSOURI. It was Faith Promise Sunday and Dan Betzer was guest speaker. Dan is often the Faith Promise Sunday speaker at James River. Pastor John Lindell introduced Dan as a man who has greatly impacted his life. Consider the dynamics: Dan impacts John . . . John impacts James River Church. . . James River Church impacts the world by giving $2.8 million to missions.

As I listened to Dan speak, I recognized many statements, illustrations, and testimonies found in this book. However, in the time allotted, Dan could only share about 10 percent of what he covers in his book. I thought to myself, "You folks don't know what you're missing!"

As the busy pastor of First Assembly of God in Fort Meyers, Florida, Dan can only visit a few churches annually. Yet he can still impact your life and church by sharing his thoughts and experiences through his book. He wrote this book for all the ministers, churches, and laity who want to be blessed. This book can be transforming if you will read it and implement its truths into your life and church.

The book Dan has written is a unique book on missions that is both inspirational and instructional. As a mission-minded minister, I was not only amazed by the testimonies but reminded of my own testimonies and why I, too, love missions. Allow me to share just three of those testimonies as they illustrate principles that Dan's book further develops.

1. It was Faith Promise Sunday at First Assembly of God in Des Moines in 1977. I had never heard of the Assemblies of God until my next-door neighbor invited me to go to church with him. The preaching of the Word hooked me. At that time I was a sales executive for Revlon cosmetics. The pastor announced that the next Sunday would be Faith Promise Sunday. I didn't have

a clue what that meant but I wanted to find out! The next Sunday, at the end of the service they read aloud how much each person had promised to give: $360, $1200, $700, $5,000, $12,000. Wow! This was more exciting than selling lipstick! I was in a place where people had found a cause in which to invest their time, their money, and their lives. I was compelled to make my first faith promise: $500! Last Sunday my wife and I promised to do more—inspired by Dan.

2. In 1985 at the New Testament Assembly of God in Millville, Pennsylvania, I was the pastor of a church that had never had a missions convention. I organized the first one. Dale Preiser, the late great missionary to Haiti, was our speaker. At the beginning of the service he asked me what our goal was. "We didn't set a goal, Dale." "You have to set a goal, Scott." Imagine it's your first missions convention and you have to set a goal . . . now! "Okay, well, the Devil's number is 666 so God's number must be 777. Dale, our mission-giving goal is $777 per month."

   Dale preached an inspired message, and we handed out faith promise cards. The church secretary set up an adding machine on the platform. I put a mic near it so everyone could hear it. The cards started coming in. "$120 a year, $300, $1,000, $60 . . ." Finally, the secretary entered the last card. I asked him to divide the total by twelve. He handed me the total: exactly $777 per month! Dale and I jumped and yelled and whooped it up like crazy men. Joy filled the house, and a church that had struggled for years became a blessed church.

3. In 1998, when I became the pastor of Park Crest Assembly of God in Springfield, Missouri, the church was over $600,000 in debt. It was a financial challenge to make the required payment each month. We deter-

mined to focus on missions like never before. In the next four years we tripled our giving to missions. Can you guess what else happened? We liquidated that loan . . . in four years! We had a mortgage shredding! As Dan writes often, God will be indebted to no one.

A blessed church makes missions their primary focus. A blessed church expects the Spirit to be at work in the details of their church life. I encourage you to read Dan's book with great expectation to hear the insights, wisdom, and creativity that the Spirit will whisper in your ear. Put Dan Betzer's principles to work and watch God bless your life and your church.

**—Scott Temple, director, Office of Ethnic Relations,
The General Council of the Assemblies of God**

INTRODUCTION

A YOUNG, VISITING PASTOR BURST INTO MY OFFICE RECENTLY, BURDENED DOWN WITH A TAPE RECORDER, IPAD, PEN AND PENCILS, AND WHAT LOOKED LIKE A REAM OF PAPER. He was so excited! He had driven hundreds of miles to ply me with questions about the seeming mystery: "Pastor Betzer, how come First Assembly of God in Fort Myers is so blessed?" His eyes lit up with eagerness as he awaited what he thought would be a deeply profound response. He sank into his chair in dismay when I answered simply, "Missions."

"No, no, Pastor. I don't want to hear that. I didn't drive hundreds of miles to hear about missions. Come on now, what's the 'Open, Sesame'? How come thousands of people attend this church? How come you're not in debt? How did you build a multi-million dollar, state-of-the-art children's center debt-free? How can you be on local television every day and national television each week . . . and not be begging for money on the air? What's the secret, Pastor? Please, tell me!"

I looked at him for a moment, smiled, and again responded, "Missions." Well, I had to tell him the truth! I only know what God has revealed to my spirit and what I have experienced through the decades.

"But . . . but, Pastor Betzer, the miracles that have taken place are known in a lot of places! Please, I know there has to be a great secret that only a handful of you guys know about. Won't you share it with me?"

"Son, I've told you. Let me tell you again: 'Missions'."

In a few minutes I watched the young fellow climb into his car and drive away, truly deflated by what he had heard. I knew he figured he had wasted his time, but had he allowed the Holy Spirit to birth in his heart what He birthed in mine a long time ago, and continues to reinforce even now, that young pastor could have entered into the greatest opportunity he ever dreamed possible.

Now I've been around for a long time. We've had twelve fine general superintendents in the Assemblies of God since our fellowship was birthed in 1914, and I have had the joy of knowing or working with eight of them. I was licensed to preach in the Assemblies of God over sixty years ago and ordained in 1962. Mainly because of my exposure as the speaker on the national radio broadcast *Revivaltime* for nearly seventeen years, I received many invitations to speak across the country and even around the world. As a result, it has been my pleasure and privilege to preach in well over a thousand churches.

Most of them were from my own fellowship, but others were congregations of other well-known denominations. Terrific ones, I might add. Some of those congregations were flourishing. It seemed almost as if God was standing over them, pouring out a Niagara of blessings. People flocked to those churches from near and far. They seemed to have enough funds to function effectively. I found them to be vibrant, relevant, and fulfilled in the work of God.

But other churches were stagnant, in debt, half-empty, out of touch with today's world, and seemingly mired in ecclesiastical quicksand. It was "gloom, despair, and agony on me," as those country boys used to sing on the television program *Hee Haw*. These congregations seemingly were going nowhere. I would go back to my hotel room and ponder why some churches were so blessed and others obviously were not.

I've witnessed many followers of Jesus who seemed to be joyful and fulfilled in the work of God, while others were sour, cantankerous, and doleful. I had to wonder why some individuals were flourishing while others were not.

We could suggest many reasons for abundance at the church level: leadership, location, music program, media coverage, etc. However, some of the "lean" and unhappy churches had all those qualities, yet were still struggling. Other "fat," forward-moving churches were located on unfamiliar streets (you almost needed Pocahontas to find them!), had less-than-stellar music, no media, and less-than-eloquent pastors, yet they were soaring and thriving. The answer to my search didn't jump out at me at first, but I kept seeking because I knew there had to be a reason.

Long ago, the Lord opened my eyes to the answer. That's what this book is about. Simply put, this is the question: Why are some churches blessed and others are not? I believe God has given me insight to that question. Please bear with me! This is most definitely not a how-to book. Methods aren't generally transferable. Activities I describe here were terrific for the churches I pastored, but they might backfire on you. Remember the classic example in 1 Samuel 17:39: Saul's armor was satisfactory for the king but it didn't work for young David. In fact, just the opposite—that iron coat might have gotten the shepherd boy killed on the battlefield.

Of necessity, I will refer to methods God has employed through my ministry that have resulted in supernatural provision. These include miraculous testimonies. I will tell you how God used these methods and activities, but I will also hasten to add that those same methods might fail you miserably unless God is in them. The Enemy might beat you half to death if you tried them.

No, it's the scriptural principles that I want to spotlight. Two of them: biblical faith and strict obedience to the commands of Jesus. Both faith and obedience are part and parcel of our Lord's explicit command to "go into all the world and preach the gospel to every creature" (Mark 16:15).

During the recent one-hundredth anniversary of the Assemblies of God, I encountered John Bueno, lifelong missionary in Latin America and former executive director of world missions for the Assemblies of God. He said, "Well, Dan, I see you're still at it, beating the drum for missions!" I responded, "John, I don't see anywhere in Scripture that I was given an exemption." He smiled as he walked away and responded over his shoulder, "You're right about that, Dan!"

It's my fervent prayer and concern that as you read this book a new dimension of faith will arise in your heart, whether you're a pastor, singer, usher, parking lot attendant or whatever in your local church. Just before He ascended back to His Father, Jesus promised: 17

"But you shall receive power when the Holy Spirit has come upon you; and you shall be witnesses to Me in Jerusalem, and in all Judaea and Samaria, and to the end of the earth" (Acts 1:8).

You and I are still living in the unfinished "twenty-ninth chapter of Acts," that sacred book that constitutes God's template for the church. May you be blessed as an individual follower of our Lord Jesus. May your church be blessed beyond measure, supernaturally so.

CHAPTER  ONE

ONE ASTOUNDING NIGHT
IN NOVEMBER

THE CROWD BEGAN ASSEMBLING IN OUR FLORIDA
SANCTUARY A FULL HOUR BEFORE THE ANNOUNCED
STARTING TIME. The parking lot was filled and attendants were
assisting late-comers to park on the grass or on nearby streets. The
sun had just set over the Gulf of Mexico and street lights were popping
on across the church property.

Over 200 members of the church music and drama department
were putting the finishing touches on their opening theme. Various
members of the cast had been in makeup for several hours to the point
where, when I saw them, I had no idea who they were. They would be
representing many nations and cultures that night.

In my study, those who would be speaking had joined me in
prayer: former Missouri governor, senator, and United States attorney
general, John Ashcroft; David Green, founder and CEO of Hobby
Lobby; ninety-two-year-old Dois Rosser, founder of International
Cooperating Ministries (and perhaps the world's foremost church
builder); Reinhard Bonnke, world-renowned evangelist; Assemblies
of God Archbishop Barnabas Mtokambali of Tanzania, Africa; local
Christian businessman, Dr. John Patrick; and myself.

My good friend, Bob D'Andrea, founder of the Christian
Television Network, had committed all of his stations as well as live
coverage coast-to-coast on both DirectTV and Dish Satellite networks

for the entire evening to televise the service—at his own expense. A few minutes before starting time, his helicopter landed in our church parking lot, only intensifying the drama.

We had billed the evening as "The Great Commission World Summit." The goal was to raise millions of dollars in one night to build churches around the world through the extraordinary ministry of ICM, the aforementioned International Cooperating Ministry. The founder, Dois Rosser, over the past several decades had constructed well over 4,000 church buildings around the world. A successful businessman, when he was in his sixties, God gave him a plan for this ministry, backed by leveraged giving and coupled with a commitment from each of those congregations to plant five churches within the next three years. As a result, Rosser now had a worldwide network of gospel-preaching churches numbering nearly 30,000. He and his staff have distributed hundreds of thousands of Bible studies as well as solar-powered gizmos (the size of a cell phone) that contain a complete Bible and a four-year Bible school course.

We were pumped! I don't know when I had ever felt such excitement coursing through a congregation. There was a buzz all over our town. Nothing of this magnitude had ever been attempted before, at least in our neck of the woods. Weeks of prayer and intercession preceded the night, as we are well aware that God only blesses what comes from Him.

I've always believed that any endeavor we undertake for Jesus is a command performance. Only our very best is ever good enough for Him.

In the months prior to that service, I lay awake many nights wondering, *Will anyone come? Can we fill the 2,000 seat sanctuary? Can we reach our goal of millions of dollars raised for building churches overseas? Will anyone truly care? Have we bitten off more than we can chew?* But I knew God had led us to undertake this mission. In God's work, faith is a necessity (more about that later in this book). We weren't doing this for our sakes. We were doing this for God in direct obedience to His Great Commission, which is not a suggestion but a command!

As a pastor, I've always believed that any endeavor we undertake for Jesus is a command performance. Only our very best is ever good enough for Him. After all, God gave us the best He had when He "so loved the world that He gave His only begotten Son, that whoever believes in Him should not perish but have everlasting life" (John 3:16). How could we make our missions convention a mediocre activity? So we spared no effort in our preparation, although we had limited funds to underwrite the night.

Can you believe that each of those speakers flew in at his own expense and didn't ask for an honorarium? John Ashcroft evoked laughter from the crowd when he opened his remarks by saying, "When Pastor Betzer called me and asked me if I believed in free speech, I didn't know he was going to ask me to make one!" What a lineup of speakers!

At five minutes before 7 p.m. the speakers and I filed into the sanctuary. The orchestra was already playing (missions music, I hasten to add!). At 7 o'clock the screens lit up with scenes from around the world. The one-hundred-voice choir began to sing and another hundred people filed through the sanctuary dressed in various international costumes (as were each of the choir members). Everyone looked awesome! The theme for the night was "All the Nations." For over ten minutes the choir sang with deep anointing as the live panorama of the actors and dancers portrayed the impact of the lyrics:

> *To You belong all the nations;*
> *To You belong all the peoples.*
> *To You belong all the kingdoms.*
> *To You belong all the tribes,*
> *Created for Your glory.*
> *We come to testify!*
>
> *Every culture, every race, find expression within this place.*
> *Every culture, every race find expression to give Him praise.*

21

Now people marched in who represented the nations of the world from north to south, east to west, crisscrossing the building and stage as the choir continued:

To You belong all the islands,
The nations that surround
within this rim of fire.
We're tearing strongholds down.
Every people, every tongue, crying out to the Holy One.
Every people, every tongue crying out, "Lord, Your kingdom come!"

By this time the sanctuary was a kaleidoscope of color, national dances, and glorious sound; the crowd responded with "amen" and applause. Across the sanctuary you could sense a rising tide of expectancy for what God was going to do among us.

Every motion, every song, every rhythm to You alone;
Every motion, every song, every rhythm before Your throne.[1]

Our staff had created a twenty-foot long, fiery red dragon, representing some of the eastern nations. The crowd oohed and aahed as the creature writhed its way through the sanctuary (operated with a few people beneath the reptile's skin). Overhead, professionals swung back and forth over the congregation on specially-hung silk draperies, up and down with dazzling maneuvers, keeping the crowd's attention firmly fixed on what was happening before them.

By the time the opening production number ended, the crowd was on its feet. Many people in attendance at our church for the first time quickly understood that we mean business when it comes to missions! To us, missions is not some second-rate, last-minute adventure in mediocrity. If it's important to God, it must be important to the local church.

Then our speakers opened their hearts, each one imploring the congregation to get their eyes on a lost and hopeless world. Pointedly they emphasized that Christ's anointed body, the church, can do something about that lost condition through the power of the Holy Spirit; after all, that's why He was poured out on the day of Pentecost. After an hour and forty-five minutes, I went to the pulpit to receive the offering, every penny of it to build churches. We closed with a congregational mission anthem, prayed, and began to make our way home. We had done everything we knew to do . . . now we would await the results.

Eighteen Months Later

From that one evening, here are the results:

- Sixty-two churches have been constructed (or are currently under construction) in eighteen countries: Burkina Faso, Dominican Republic, Egypt, India, Russia, Bangladesh, Bolivia, Chile, Ecuador, Ethiopia, Guatemala, Kenya, Sri Lanka, Liberia, Myanmar, Mozambique, Nicaragua, and Peru
- The congregations that benefitted from The Great Commission World Summit have already begun the great evangelistic task of planting 310 more churches
- Twenty thousand new believers have been reached for Christ

That's the results for the kingdom of God from just one night! One night! It's astounding what Holy Spirit-filled believers can do, realizing again and again in the most practical ways ever dreamed that we have received power after the Holy Ghost has come upon us! Yes! We have received power, supernatural capacity to fulfill what God has commanded us. You won't find expressions such as "We can't do that" or "We can't afford that" in the book of Acts. As the world-changing missionary-apostle Paul reminded us: "I can do all things through Christ who strengthens me" (Phil. 4:13).

That was just one night. There's so much more to this story. Our church in Florida is made up of ordinary people, just as most congregations are. You won't see Bentley or Rolls-Royce vehicles in our church parking lot. You will see Toyotas and Chevys and Jeeps. But in the past twenty-five years or so, as of this writing, these committed saints have given over thirty-seven million dollars to global evangelism at home and abroad. They have planted over eight churches in Florida, mostly in our area.

Perhaps someone is protesting, "Well . . . a church that large can do things like that; but our congregation is small. What can *we* do to make a difference?"

Great question! Let me explain to you that my passionate love for the task of missions began when I was starting home-mission churches in Ohio back in the '60s. Everything I learned about giving to missions I learned in those churches, where we had few people and virtually no money. We started one of those churches in the basement of our rented home where my pulpit was a Maytag washer-dryer.

But God intervened! In the most dramatic and highly unexpected ways, the Lord brought people into my life who revolutionized my thinking. The Holy Spirit, the fabulous teacher whom Jesus said would come to us, brought into my life circumstances that gave me insight into ministry and missions I had never heard of—and probably would never have dreamed of. These people and circumstances radically raised the bar on my faith expectations.

I want to tell you the story of how it all began—and why it continues. As Paul Harvey used to say, "Now you will know the rest of the story!"

CHAPTER  **TWO**

GOD'S EMISSARY FROM CANADA

I WAS BROUGHT UP IN A CHRISTIAN HOME. We lived in the thriving town of Climbing Hill, Iowa, population 112. My parents were saved in 1936 following the death of their firstborn child, who lived a mere four days. His cemetery marker reads simply, "Baby Boy Betzer." That tragic occurrence somehow brought my parents into contact with a great pastor and church that met in a primitive tabernacle-type structure with sawdust on the floor. The building was located twenty-five miles from Climbing Hill in the west end of Sioux City, Iowa. The pastor, Willis Smith, was a man of marvelous faith.

My parents' conversion was remarkable. To this day I'm convinced that only the supernatural action of God could have brought about their faith. Willis Smith prayed over my dying twenty-year-old cousin while she was breathing her last in a cancerous coma. The doctor said she would never recover, but Smith prayed that God would raise her from that death bed. Several days later, Faye left the hospital and lived another forty years of productive ministry. That miracle caught the attention of most of our relatives, and so our family was spiritually born in that atmosphere of faith.

My father was a barber by trade. Oh, how he and Mom loved the Lord. Jesus had done so much for them! My father and mother became "pillars" in that old church. Dad became a Sunday school superintendent and board member who was steadfastly loyal to God and the pastor. I never heard my father express a single negative word about the pastor or the church. I was blessed to have faithful pastors during my childhood and teen years; I received solid training in the Bible both from them and remarkable Sunday school teachers. Now that I think of it, I don't recall ever missing Sunday school or church, even on Wednesday nights, unless I was seriously ill. And I don't recall my father ever *asking* me if I would like to go to church. No, it was, "Get in the car, Danny. It's church time." That wasn't a problem for me; I loved our church and our pastors.

Northwest Iowa can often get clobbered by snow. I remember those brutal winters with their withering blasts sweeping down from the north. Some might have said, "Well, we can't make it to church today. The snow's too deep." But my Dad would put chains on our 1932 Chevy, and off we went to church, sliding across those snow-covered Iowa gravel roads, up and down the rolling country hills. My parents ingrained in me faithfulness to the house of God. What a heritage!

I spent my first year of college in Bible school where anointed teachers poured the life of the Scriptures into my young heart. Their classes were most helpful in formulating my ministerial life; however, I don't recall being taught much about missions, with the exception of one godly professor who had served for decades in India. Occasionally, our church would host a missionary, but these appearances were usually perfunctory. Sacrificial or priority giving to global evangelism never struck home with us. My father loved those missionaries and would sometimes invite them to our tiny 800-square-foot home for dinner. I recall sitting up as late as my folks would allow, listening to those men and women speak glowingly about their call to a foreign field. Dad would always find a way to give money to each of them.

In college I met the lovely lady who would become my bride, Darlene Laura Beem (whose father was a pastor in Nebraska and later became the director and business manager for *Revivaltime*, the network radio program of the Assemblies of God). Darlene and I were married in July of 1956 at just nineteen years of age. As of this writing, we've been married over fifty-eight years.

We knew God had called us into ministry, and after a period of waiting upon Him for several years He opened the door for us to begin fulfilling that call. My initial response to the Lord's call on my life was to pray: "I'll go anywhere you want me to go—except the North. (Remember I was raised in northwest Iowa, and I never wanted to see snow again!) And I'll do anything you ever ask me to do—except pioneer churches." The moral of the story is: be careful what you tell God you will or won't do. Making such stipulations to Him is not unlike drawing on the Lone Ranger! In fact, I remember asking the Lord for a beach ministry. God answered the prayer, just not in the way I anticipated. Darlene and I spent the next decade or so pioneering churches on a beach alright—the south beach of Lake Erie in central Ohio. Our first day in pastoral ministry there was in January of 1962, smack in the middle of a blizzard. Snow was stacked everywhere. It seemed to me as we drove into the town, that I could hear celestial laughter . . . but it was probably just my imagination.

Sandusky, Ohio, was a town of about 35,000 citizens, halfway between Cleveland and Toledo. Darlene and I felt a definite call from God to begin a full-gospel work there in the '60s. We had no backing or financial support, humanly speaking. I never thought we needed any if God ordained our call. We experienced a tough start. We rented a high school auditorium for thirty nights, selling almost everything we had to raise the funds. Cold, lots of snow, miserable surroundings, a total lack of interest among the people we were trying to reach, and a definite lack of funds made me wonder if I had somehow missed God's call. In fact, the biggest crowd I remember in the first couple weeks was sixteen people. Hardly a noteworthy beginning!

One day, in deep despondency, I called the legendary pastor/evangelist Rex Humbard in Akron where he pastored the famed Cathedral of Tomorrow. I asked if I could come see him. He warmly invited me to do so, right away, in fact. When I arrived, I was ushered into his study where he graciously received me. I poured out my heart to him. I reported that I knew God had called us to Sandusky and Erie County, but the work was going nowhere. Sixteen attendees that included my family of four hardly solicited rising expectations on my part. Rex listened intently to every word. I was shocked when he responded, "You go back to Sandusky and tell the people that my wife and I are coming, along with all my music staff (which included the original Cathedral quartet), and we'll hold a service in your rented auditorium a week from Saturday night." I backed away and said, "Oh, sir, we have no money! I can't even cover your gasoline costs to get there." Rex laughed and said, "We don't want your money. We'll sing and preach and give an altar call for the lost to come to Christ, and then I'll raise an offering to help you get started in your church. The converts that night will be potential members of your new church."

Rex did exactly what he said he would do. There were nearly a thousand people who attended that Saturday night because the Humbards were so well-known in Ohio. The offering was several thousand dollars, and Rex gave us the entire amount. He didn't keep a dime for himself or his ministry in Akron. And some folks came to Christ in his altar call for salvation who did, indeed, begin to attend our church. Until the day he died, I tried to thank Rex in every way I knew how. He gave me one of my earliest lessons on how to be a blessing and how to give unconditionally.

After about a year, we had ninety people in our little church and were settled in a cute chapel on a main thoroughfare. But here's the rub: Our entire church budget (and remember this was back in the '60s) was $16,000 annually—over $300 per week in tithes and offerings! This covered our mortgage, my salary, supplies, outreach, you name it. The problem was we rarely exceeded $200 in weekly giving. I would preach on tithing and would hear "amen" from the congregation; but when the offering plate was passed—nothing! Every week we still collected the same $200 or so. Something was terribly wrong. I couldn't figure it out. I couldn't reconcile what God had called us to do with the lack of funding. Hadn't God promised to meet every need? So where was the divine provision?

After the first year, we were over $5,000 dollars in the red in general fund offerings. Obviously, a church can't go into debt indefinitely. We had bills to pay, and we didn't have the money. No, it wasn't a great amount of money, but the bills added up. I would get bills in the mail followed up by a few phone calls, "When can you pay us, Pastor?" It was like getting nibbled to death by a duck. I don't handle financial pressure well and, as a result, I became very ill. I was sick for several weeks, fretting about this church's financial dilemma for which I had no answer.

One day as I was recovering and asking the Lord about the lack of money, I felt Him speak to me almost as if it were audible. (It wasn't audible or I might've had a heart attack! But, believe me, I knew it was the Lord!) I had been questioning God about my call to Sandusky and the lack of funds. "Lord, I've done everything I know to do. What's my problem?" Here is the gist of what I felt God say to me in my spirit: *"I haven't responded to your prayers for help, Dan, because you're not in the same business I'm in! You do what I'm doing, and I'll supply your need."*

I was shocked. "What? Are you kidding me, Lord? Not in the same business? Why, I study and pray, I preach sermons, I teach Sunday school, we have a cute little building that actually looks like a church, we print a bulletin—what do you mean I'm not in the same business you're in? Why . . . I'm even ordained!"

The Lord continued: *"Dan, what are you doing about reaching the world with the gospel? Do you ever preach about missions? Do you ever tell the congregation that, like Paul, they are debtors to all people? Do you have missionaries speak at the church? Do you send funds for global evangelism? My business is to reach every person on this planet! How are you doing with that? Dan, answer Me—is missions your priority? It was My priority before the beginning of the world; that's why I gave My only begotten Son to humanity. Now what are you doing about it? Are you interested in doing what I'm doing?"*

I sputtered, "Well now, Lord . . . You know we don't have any money. We can hardly pay our utility bill. We have to scrimp on things to pay the mortgage. We don't have money for missionaries. That's what I've been trying to tell you! We're broke! We surely can't afford missionaries, too."

Next came the shocker: *"Dan, I don't really have much interest in your building, your utilities, or anything else you've made your priority. My Son died to save the lost of the entire world, and you're not getting the Word out. You aren't implementing My divine plan, and you're not obeying the Great Commission of going into all the world to preach the gospel. You see, Dan, it's not just about reaching your 'Jerusalem'—Sandusky. It's about reaching every nation, and you're ignoring the command or at least hiding behind your excuse of lack of funding. Now you make global missions your priority in this church and I'll take care of your bills."*

The Lord gave me a set of three directions that would forever change my ministry.

I certainly had never heard anything like that before, and it scared me! Then the Lord gave me a set of three directions that would forever change my ministry. (Please bear in mind that God may not direct every pastor or church leader with the same methods He demanded of me; but He will require a plan! And I can almost guarantee it will scare you.)

1. Have an Annual Missionary Convention

Oh, how I protested that one! A missionary convention, indeed! Every missionary convention I had ever attended was boring. The insomniac's special! Back in those days, missionaries would usually come to a church with a slide presentation. Remember them? Now, if there's anything duller than slides I don't know what it is, unless it's eating Spam. I was present in a service one night when a missionary presented his pictures. The house lights were turned down and, with a little clicker in his hand, he rotated through the pictures: "Here's a picture of some trees in Africa." Click. "Here are some more trees." Click. "And way off in the distance you can see some huts under a tree." And on and on . . . until the highlight picture: Click, "This is a picture of my wife and our pet chimpanzee. My wife is the one on the right." I kid you not! That's exactly what he said. Well, that ended that service for me. The congregation roared with laughter. The poor fellow never regained control of that service.

Then there was the obligatory last slide: "Here we see the sun setting into the sea. Darkness is replacing the light. It's spiritually dark all over the world, and we must spread the light." That was certainly true—it was just a boring and 100 percent predictable way to present that reality. When the houselights finally came back on, a number of the saints had settled in for a long winter's nap.

I complained to the Lord, "Missionary conventions are so boring." And the Lord responded, *"Dan, I will teach you how to have a real convention, and it will never be dull, I assure you. In fact, your annual missionary convention will become the motor of your church."* So I acquiesced reluctantly, "Okay, Lord. I'll have a Sunday where we emphasize missions." To which God responded, *"No, Dan—in your case, I want you to dedicate eight days, an entire week with two Sundays to your convention! I want this to be the major factor in the congregation."* I gulped and said, "Okay." I've obeyed that order now for decades with startling results. The annual missionary convention truly is *"the motor of our church."* And we bill it as such.

2. Have Dr. Oswald J. Smith as Your Convention Speaker

In spite of being sick, I laughed out loud. Have Dr. Oswald J. Smith as our convention speaker? I thought to myself, *Why, sure. And I'll have the Marine Marching Band play the offertory and Frank Sinatra sing some of his favorite hymns! How in the world would I get such a renowned figure to come to our dinky church?* Again the Lord responded, "Ask him."

Ask him? Ask this incredible stalwart of the church to grace our miniature chapel? Just ask him? Oh, how many blessings we miss when we pass over God's directions as too simplistic—or impossible. But I had a reason for my skepticism. When Smith passed away in 1986 at the age of ninety-seven, Billy Graham proclaimed at his funeral, "I have lost a dear friend, the man who had more impact on my life than any other—a great preacher, a great songwriter, a man who stands 31 equal with Moody and Torrey. As a missionary statesman he stands alone. There was no equal."[2]

Graham was certainly right in his assessment. Over a span of eighty years of ministry, Smith preached over twelve thousand sermons in eighty nations. He wrote thirty-five books as well as over one thousand two hundred of our finest gospel hymns. He was the author of such popular standards as "Fairest of Ten Thousand Is Jesus" and "Then Jesus Came." He made twenty-one world tours telling multitudes about Christ. For decades he pastored the historic People's Church in Toronto, Canada. This was the man God wanted me to invite to our tiny church in Ohio.

But God said to do it, so I wrote to Dr. Smith asking him to be the main speaker at our November, 1968, missionary convention. Imagine my surprise when He contacted me immediately and said he felt God had called him to invest almost a week into my life and that of our little church. I was so taken back by his letter. I shouldn't have been, for God had said to invite him, but I was. How many victories do we miss simply because we don't believe what God says.

3. Have a Missions Faith Promise Goal of $20,000

By this time I wasn't just ill, I was choking! Twenty thousand dollars? I tried to explain to the Lord, "Our whole annual budget is $16,000, and we aren't coming close to that! How in the world could we ever think about a mission commitment like $20,000? That would be $400 a week just for missions! That's impossible! It's absolutely, categorically impossible!"

The reason I thought that way is because no one had ever explained "faith promise giving" to me. I didn't even know what a mission pledge was! (It's not just a matter of semantics. We'll discuss these things in more detail in later chapters.)

I was about to see something happen that I couldn't have dreamed possible prior to God's instructions to me. I knew one thing: Neither I nor our little congregation had ever believed for anything

like that! Twenty thousand dollars . . . for missions? In one year? Why
. . . why . . . it would have to be supernatural!

As soon as I was well enough to return to work, I called the
church board together and explained to them what I have just written
to you. God bless those dear people, they responded immediately,
"Pastor, if that's what you believe, let's go for it." They weren't terribly
convincing in the way they expressed their agreement, but at least
they gave it.

Over the next several months we fit together the pieces of the
upcoming convention and the arrival of Dr. Smith. We didn't know
it yet, but we were in for the ride of our lives. I was about to learn a
divine lesson that I've never forgotten. I would never have believed,
not even for a moment, what I was to experience that week. There's no
doubt about it—the congregation and I were about to have an "entrée
into the supernatural!"

CHAPTER  THREE

ENTRÉE INTO THE SUPERNATURAL

I BELIEVE THE BIBLE IS LITERALLY TRUE. If I didn't, I wouldn't spend a single day in the ministry. My firm rock is God's infallible Word—all of it. As a result, I must take what Jesus said at face value, or I lose all credibility. In His last moments with His disciples, prior to His ascension, Jesus told them: "But you will receive power when the Holy Spirit has come upon you; and you shall be witnesses to me in Jerusalem, and in all Judaea and Samaria, and to the end of the earth" (Acts 1:8).

What did the Lord promise? Power! "You will receive power." Over the past fifty-five years, I've had the privilege of preaching in hundreds of congregations across America and around the world. I sometimes leave those services wondering, *Where's the power? They claim here to be Pentecostal, but where is the supernatural? What's the difference between that church and a civic club?* There's nothing wrong with a good civic club; I belonged to one for years and enjoyed it. But those organizations deal with the *natural* world. There's no question they often do a lot of good in a community. The clubs meet regularly. Sometimes they sing when they get together. They often collect dues or other funds for projects. The club members frequently eat together in fellowship, right?

Well the same may be said for many churches. We meet, take up an offering, eat together sometimes, and do good for those around us. But as Peggy Lee used to sing, "Is that all there is?"[3] The church should be—must be—undergirded by the supernatural. That statesman of preachers, Stephen Olford, long-time pastor of Calvary Baptist Church in New York City, once said in my hearing, "The only rationale for Christ's church is the supernatural!" The supernatural? Then . . . where is it?

Let's face it: We church leaders often make decisions based on:

- Can we afford it?
- Is this budgeted?
- Do we have a slush fund for emergencies?
- Will this appeal to everyone in the congregation?
- Will we lose or gain people pursuing this action?

The call of God sometimes seems beside the point in some of these churches, and the dollar becomes the criteria for obedience to God. This is especially true when it comes to missions. For example, when America suffered the recession in 2008, what was often the first thing cut from the budget in many churches? Missionary support! In this book I will prove to you from Scripture that such action immediately clogs up the divine supply line. In our little church in Sandusky back in the '60s, we hadn't taken much note of the Great Commission, and I can assure you that the financial pipeline from heaven was thoroughly stopped up. In fact, our finances redefined the word *clogged*.

The Beginning of the Beginning

The day before our first missionary convention, after a lot of hard work and prayer from many of the ninety or so people in the church, I drove to Cleveland Hopkins airport to pick up Dr. Oswald J. Smith. I had never met the man or even talked on the phone with him, so I had no idea what to expect. Back in those days, airport security was minimal, and we could still go to the gates to meet our guests. That was helpful because I wanted to see Smith before he saw me.

I watched the Air Canada plane pull up to the gate and noticed an elderly gentleman emerge from the jet and walk somewhat sprightly down the steps. He was quite thin, I noted. The breeze blew his shock of snow-white hair hither and yon as he walked to the gate. I guessed him to be about five feet, ten inches tall. When he entered the concourse I approached him warily and introduced myself, quite unaware of the enormous impact this man would make on my life.

Smith wasn't a particularly approachable fellow. I couldn't engage him in much small talk. It always seemed to me that his mind was somewhere else or he was listening to music no other mortal could hear. This in no way negated the incredible way he affected my life, but that wouldn't begin to happen until the following Tuesday. Driving back to Sandusky I told my guest about the week we had planned, and he seemed alright with our plans—not beside himself with eagerness but agreeable. I thought God had sent this man into my life to encourage me; I couldn't imagine how much he would anger me first.

We had promoted the missions convention in every way we knew how and, as a result, the opening night was quite full. Our small sanctuary would seat several hundred persons. I was on pins and needles as this was all new stuff to me. I didn't know exactly what to expect. I think I was hoping for Smith to be a mover and shaker, a motivator

> "What right do you have to hear the gospel over and over when so many have never heard it for the first time?"

who would bring people roaring to their feet. You know, rah, rah, rah! That is definitely not what we experienced. Oh boy, is that *not* what we got!

After singing some songs about missions, I introduced Smith to the crowd. He approached our pulpit, stood there quietly for a few minutes, and then took us to the proverbial woodshed. "What did you want from me?" he asked. "How many times have you heard the gospel? How many church services have you attended? Were you expecting something new from me?" Then he dropped the bomb: "What right do you have to hear the gospel over and over when so many have never heard it for the first time? What makes you so special?" The crowd was shocked into silence. And it got even worse. The crowd was stunned . . . and so was I. In the first sixty seconds Smith had torn us to pieces. Quite frankly, many of the folks were glaring. Oh, not at Smith—at *me!*

Like a man drowning, I felt my life race in front of my eyes. To make matters worse, I faced the prospect of spending an entire week with this aggravating old man. Thoughts of the service the next night surged through my brain. Monday night + missions + Smith: now there's a combination for you. We'd be fortunate if three people showed up: Darlene, me, and Smith. And I wasn't sure about Darlene! *Lord, what have you done to me?* I questioned in my heart. Darlene was sitting by the piano. I looked her way and mouthed one word, "Pack!" I knew the Betzers would be leaving Sandusky very soon.

Smith's entire message was foreign to all of us. He quoted Scripture, he cited evangelism experiences from around the world, and threw out challenges that stunned us. Oh, I knew that the next night, Monday, would be grim.

I must admit I was extremely angry with Smith. I was expecting a motivator, not a put-down expert! I wanted him to challenge the folks, not skin them alive. We didn't speak much on the way back to his motel room. I was burning up inside. But if Smith noticed, he didn't seem bothered. There are some people who just hear different music. They aren't entangled by what people think about them. Like Paul, they claim, "None of these things move me" (Acts 20:24). After a perfunctory "goodnight," we parted, and I drove home to a sleepless night.

I knew Monday would be a long, long day . . . and it was. The phone calls started coming in early, but surprisingly, the callers weren't angry. Some folks dropped by my tiny office to chat about Smith's approach, but they didn't seem stressed out. The same couldn't be said for me. I was . . . what's the ecclesiastical term I'm looking for here—oh yes, *torqued!*

The following evening, I drove Smith back to the church in virtual silence. It seemed like ten miles from the motel to our church, although it was only a few blocks. Then an amazing thing happened. Approaching our little church, about thirty minutes before the scheduled start of the service, I was startled to see that the parking lot was full. No, of course it wasn't a big lot, but it was jammed! The fellow who oversaw our parking stopped my car, and I rolled down the window to see what he wanted. He said, "Pastor, give me your keys, and I'll park your car for you. We had to use your space."

I asked him, "Why are all these cars here?"

He replied, "The church is full."

I asked him again, "Why?"

He replied, "I'm not sure what has happened, but we're putting chairs down the aisles."

Chairs down the aisle? I couldn't imagine it. Had some of those folks come with ropes and guns? Why had the crowd grown? Did our people approach their friends to ask, "Want to come to our church tonight and have your skin ripped off?" Where did all these people come from? Was I pastoring a church made up of masochists?

We entered the church through the back door, and I peeked past the platform to discover the parking lot attendant was right. There were people everywhere. In instant gratitude I thought to myself, *Oh, Lord, thank you for giving Dr. Smith the opportunity to pour on the oil tonight and make things smoother and more comfortable.* Wrong! Smith was worse that night. He was almost brutal in confronting us with our lack of obedience to the Great Commission. Once again I felt my ministerial career coming to a screeching halt.

On Tuesday night, not only was the sanctuary packed but the ushers had to set up chairs in the small lobby area. Even on Easter we had never had a congregation like that! I often wonder if people don't get weary of spiritual pablum and long for the solid meat of the Word and true challenges from God. We often hear ministers "share," but what would happen if they "declared"? That night, in that God-ordained service, radically changed my life. The congregation would be changed by the Holy Spirit before the night was over, but not as changed as I would be!

Former heavyweight champ Evander Holyfield once told me that he could never be knocked out by any punch he saw coming. Well . . . I never saw the punch coming.

CHAPTER ✿ **FOUR**

SELL MY CAR?

D R. SMITH WAS SUPER ANOINTED AS HE PRESENTED THE CHALLENGE OF MISSIONS THAT TUESDAY NIGHT. The audience sat transfixed as the grand old man, so used of God around the world, opened his heart to them. He pulled no punches, each night of the week increasing our realization that we followers of Christ are truly "debtors" to Jew and Greek. "I am a debtor both to Greeks and to barbarians, both to wise and to unwise" (Rom. 1:14).

Even as I listened intently to Smith's challenge, I could occasionally hear a muffled sob coming from those assembled or the shuffling of feet in the packed congregation. The Holy Spirit had our attention, and He was bringing the eternal truths home. Conviction hits people in different ways. There was no question the Holy Spirit was reshaping our thoughts and priorities. Paul wrote: "Christ Jesus came into the world to save sinners, of whom I am chief" (1 Tim. 1:15). And Jesus informed His disciples: "As the Father has sent Me, I also send you" (John 20:21). What has He sent us to do? To take the gospel message to sinners—everywhere in the world, not just in our hometowns.

As I sat behind Smith on the platform, I watched God deal strongly with people. Then (and I wasn't expecting this) the Lord began to deal strongly with me. I had prayed that God would influence our people in a new and powerful way, but I never dreamed the impact would primarily affect me. I would be radically changed before the night was over. And today, decades later, I'm still not over what happened that night. I should have been expecting such a thing, I suppose. I had heard church leaders say that no church can rise above the level of its leadership. So if I expected our little congregation to experience a paradigm shift concerning missions, I would have to allow the Holy Spirit to begin with me.

God Spoke to Me

As Smith preached, the Holy Spirit gently and quietly asked me, *"Dan, do you really believe what My servant is presenting here? Are you convinced I'm using him to take everyone to a new place in Me? Are you willing to encounter the supernatural in this church?"*

The supernatural? As opposed to "business as usual," I thought? Of course, I was willing, so in my spirit I answered, "Yes, Lord, of course I believe what Smith is saying to us. And I believe he is saying it as Your work through him."

Then in my spirit I heard the Lord say, *"Good. I'm glad you're in agreement with this message. Now . . . sell your car and give the money to missions."*

Wait a minute! Hold on! I wouldn't mind increasing our personal missions giving a few bucks a week, but sell my car? Not my car! See, I love cars. I truly do! When I get to heaven, I don't want wings sprouting from my back. I've done all the flying I ever need to do right down here in this earthly life. No, when I get to heaven, "Lord, how about a Bentley or a Ferrari?"

At that time I had a one-year-old Pontiac Bonneville—the big one. Long, sleek, and powerful, it was an absolutely gorgeous vehicle. I had purchased it nearly new, with thirty-six monthly payments. I had made twelve of them and had just twenty-four more to go. I pampered that car. I washed it every couple of days and kept it waxed. The interior was immaculate. Someone once said to me, "Pastor, your car is so shined up you could use one of the doors for a mirror while you're shaving!" I never splurged on anything else—but that car was my "baby." I loved it. Sell my car? That can't be the Lord. It must be acid distress. Or maybe it's the weariness of trying to get our church finances in order. God would never ask me to do anything like that. It would just kill me to sell that car. Like one comedian's version of Noah talking to God, I wanted to ask, "Is there someone else up there I could talk to?"

I took Smith back to the hotel. By this time we were talking again. But I didn't mention the car deal to him. I didn't figure it was any of his business. Or anyone else's for that matter. Then I drove home to our little parsonage. Oh, I was torn in my spirit. That divine directive to part with my dearly-loved vehicle couldn't have come from God! Surely not!

Darlene had put the kids to bed and prepared a little snack for us before we retired. Now you must understand: My wife is a beautiful woman. She has lovely blond hair (I've since turned to silver) and gorgeous brown eyes that melt my heart. She had prepared some coffee and a small dessert that we ate while discussing the phenomenal convention we were experiencing. Then, from across the table, she looked into my eyes and asked, "Dan, did God tell you to sell our car tonight? And . . . give the money to missions?"

Startled, I snapped back, "Yes, He did!"

She smiled and responded, "Well, then, we had better obey Him."

Can you conceive of such a thing? God had directed both of us to spread our faith wings.

It was tough for me to sleep that night. "Oh God, don't ask for my car. How about a sofa? Or something else?" But I knew in my heart what God was asking—requiring—of me. And I remembered what our Lord had said: "If anyone loves Me, he will keep My words; and My Father will love him, and We will come to him and make our home with him. He who does not love Me does not keep My words; and the word which you hear is not Mine but the Father's who sent Me" (John 14:23–24).

Okay, so we would sell the car. However, I reminded myself that it wasn't easy to market a car outright. So I went to our local newspaper that morning and paid for an ad to run in the classified section for five days. I cleverly put a price on that Pontiac that only a total idiot would ever pay! That would take care of the whole problem, and God could never say I didn't try to obey Him! Nobody would pay that much for that car.

Two days after the ad was published I watched the "idiot" drive away in my beautiful car. I had the money in my hand. More money than I'd ever held in my entire life. Darlene was beaming as she said, "Dan, isn't the Lord faithful?" I replied in the affirmative, although not too enthusiastically, and told her I would go to the bank and pay off the lien on the car and give what was left to missions.

Once again I got that look (that melting look) from her, and she responded, "You know, Dan, I don't think that's what God wants us to do. I think He wants us to give that entire amount to missions."

I explained to her that I couldn't legally do that because the bank was carrying a note on that car and the borrowed amount had to be satisfied. Then, with what remained, we could talk about our offering to missions. She smiled and said, "Oh, Dan, you just tell that nice bank president that we'll sign a personal promissory note on the unpaid balance. Then we can give the whole amount from the car sale to missions."

I knew that no bank president would ever do such a thing. But . . . he did. And he did it happily. "I think that's a wonderful thing you're doing, Pastor Betzer. Glad to help you!" I was shocked as I signed the personal note for the remaining amount, leaving the very healthy balance of the money for missions.

Let me interject here that several years later in 1974, our little church bought that downtown bank building, a glorious four-story, marble structure that was on the tax duplicate for $6.5 million. We bought it for $80,000! But that's a story we share in chapter 9, and even more proof that Jesus meant it when He instructed us that, "signs will follow those who believe" (Mark 16:17).

An Attitude Adjustment

Scriptures teach that God loves a cheerful giver (2 Cor. 9:7), but apparently He'll also take money from a grouch! That's exactly what I was. I had a rotten attitude about the entire episode. I missed my car! Since we were still making payments on a signature note, I didn't have the money on my meager salary to make a second monthly payment so we could buy another car. All we had to drive was a horrible, green, rusted old Rambler! A green one! An icky green one! I loathed that car. It had no power, no class, no anything. It even emitted an obnoxious odor! Every morning I climbed into that wretched machine, mumbling to myself, remembering the sleek Bonneville I had recently sold and given the money to some missionary somewhere.

Some months later I received a thick packet in the mail from the missionary who had received the money from the Pontiac. He had sent photos of the church he had built in Africa with the proceeds. It wasn't a fancy building such as one would expect in America. It was just a cement slab, steel posts, a tin roof, and cement blocks on the floor holding up planks of wood on which sat hundreds of Africans listening to the gospel. There were more pictures. Altars were filled with folks coming to Christ for salvation, healing, and the infilling of the Holy Spirit. That somewhat primitive structure and its contents had been erected from the sale of my Pontiac!

It's amazing how one's attitude can seemingly change reality. When I went to lunch that day, there was the wretched, green Rambler in the church parking lot. But wait a minute! At that moment I learned an amazing thing: When you approach a Rambler from a certain angle, allowing the sun to hit it just **We don't give to get; we give to obey. We let God deal with the aftermath in the way He chooses.** right, it looks like a . . . a Bentley! Not really, of course, but, oh, how my attitude had changed. Even now I think about that Pontiac probably rusting in a forgotten junk heap somewhere, but that church in Africa still serves as a lighthouse to hundreds of people. As I climbed into the Rambler that day, the Holy Spirit asked, "Dan, which of the two do you think I've honored the most: that church overseas or your old car?" The answer was obvious!

Now, hold on, I know what you're thinking. You're thinking God provided me with a shiny, powerful new car, right? "Why, Dan Betzer, surely God gave you a Mercedes! Right?" Uh . . . wrong. He didn't give me a car of any kind. In fact, I drove that Rambler for several more years, which wasn't a problem for me because I hadn't given the money from the Pontiac to get a new car. I had given it to obey what God had commanded us to do so we could provide funds for a missionary to present the gospel. We don't give to get; we give to obey. We let God deal with the aftermath in the way He chooses. If He replaces what we've given, that's great. If He doesn't, well, that's okay too.

The car incident was remarkable, but what happened to the little church the following weekend was even more so. The funds from the sale of the car had nothing to do with the faith promises committed by the congregation. That was something altogether separate. I was about to see the supernatural provision of God in that little church in Ohio. It was only the first of a series of financial miracles that I've witnessed since. As Alice declared in her adventures in Wonderland, it just got "curiouser and curiouser."

CHAPTER FIVE

MIRACLE OF THE FAITH PROMISE

BY THE TIME SUNDAY ROLLED AROUND, OUR LITTLE CHURCH HAD AN AURA OF EXPECTATION THAT I HAD NEVER SEEN THERE BEFORE. Our goal for missions that morning had been announced at $20,000, which humanly speaking was a ridiculous undertaking. As you may recall from an earlier chapter, our entire annual church budget was a mere $16,000—and no missions giving was included. Why not? We didn't support missionaries and their projects. Why? We didn't have the money!

I've heard it said in scores of missionary conventions and banquets through the years: "We can barely keep the church lights on! How could we ever support a missionary?" In our case in that little church, how in the whole wide world could our meager congregation ever come up with $20,000 for missions when we couldn't even supply $16,000 for the general fund? And, if we did, what would happen to our already strapped general fund giving? As I've heard from so many church leaders through the years, "Well, there's only so much blood in a turnip!" (I've searched the Bible through and through and just can't seem to find that verse.)

But during that missions convention week, Dr. Smith had taught us the biblical principles of "faith-promise giving." No, no—not a pledge! Faith-promise giving is as far removed from "a pledge" as—well, as far as a Pontiac Bonneville is from a Rambler. A pledge makes you responsible for giving such-and-such an amount; a faith promise makes God responsible. The supply depends upon Him, not us. We sing "How Great Thou Art" but blanch at a step of faith that depends upon God and Him alone. Well, is God truly great or isn't He?

A faith promise boils down to this: I believe God is great and that His divine supply is infinite, so how much can I trust Him to provide in the next twelve months to advance the message of redemption around the world? I will become a human conduit through whom He can supply funds to pass on through the local church's mission challenge.

Can I believe God for an additional $100 a month? Or for $50? Can I believe that God will run $10,000 through my hands in the next year to take the gospel to the lost of the world? The question isn't how big do I believe my bank account is but how big do I believe God is.

We never keep the faith promise cards that people fill out nor do we ask anyone for the funds throughout the coming year. We keep no records of the promises. These are between the individual and God.

In one of his books, Smith explained:

I do not believe in pledges. I have never taken up a pledge offering in my life. What is the difference, you ask, between a pledge offering and a faith promise offering? All the difference in the world. A pledge offering is between you and (the recipient). Some day (someone) will come along and try to collect it, or you may receive a letter asking for it. In other words, you can be held responsible for a pledge offering.

A faith promise offering, on the other hand, is between you and God. No one will ever ask you for it. No one will ever send you a letter reminding you of it. It is a promise made by you to God and to God alone. If you are unable to pay it, all you have to do is tell God.[4]

Let's face it, many congregations deal with missions according to the finances on hand or the local or national economy. Worse yet, they become prisoners of the "what we've always done" mentality. Their theme mantra is "We've never done it that way before." They never seem to be able to merge faith with vision. And because they can't, multitudes are condemned to a Christ-less grave and an eternity without hope.

The Faith Factor

God is clear about what He considers faith:

Now faith is the substance of things hoped for, the evidence of things not seen. For by it the elders obtained a good testimony. By faith we understand that the worlds were framed by the word of God, so that the things which are seen were not made of things which are visible. By faith Abel offered to God a more excellent sacrifice than Cain, through which he obtained witness that he was righteous, God testifying of his gifts; and through it he being dead still speaks. By faith Enoch was taken away so that he did not see death, "and was not found, because God had taken him"; for before he was taken he had this testimony, that he pleased God. But without faith it is impossible to please Him, for he who comes to God must believe that He is, and that He is a rewarder of those who diligently seek him. (Heb. 11:1–6)

Let's take a closer look at those verses. Verse 1 explains clearly that the faith God honors involves those things we hope for, long for, even though there isn't a sign of their ever coming into reality. This was Elijah praying for rain and not a single cloud appeared in the sky. When one small cloud finally appeared, the prophet told King Ahab, in effect, "Run for your life—there's going to be a gusher!"

And Elijah said to Ahab, "Go up, eat and drink; for there is the sound of abundance of rain. So Ahab went up to eat

49

and drink. And Elijah went up to the top of Carmel; then he bowed down on the ground, and put his face between his knees, and said to his servant, "Go up now, look toward the sea." So he went up, and looked, and said, "There is nothing." And seven times he said, "Go again." Then it came to pass the seventh time, that he said, "There is a cloud, as small as a man's hand, rising out of the sea!" So he said, "Go up, say to Ahab, 'Prepare your chariot, and go down before the rain stops you.'" Now it happened in the meantime that the sky became black with clouds and wind, and there was a heavy rain. So Ahab rode away and went to Jezreel. Then the hand of the LORD came upon Elijah; and he girded up his loins and ran ahead of Ahab to the entrance of Jezreel. (1 Kings 18:41–46)

Don't you just love it? For years—no rain. Then because of Elijah's faith and obedience—an *abundance* of rain!

We cannot begin to serve the Lord without faith. It just isn't possible.

Hebrews 11:3 teaches that God originally made everything He created out of nothing: "things which are seen were not made of things which are visible." The raw material the Great Creator employed then and now was . . . nothing! So when a believer or congregation complains that they have nothing to work with—voilà—they're in business. God works miracles with "nothing."

Verse 6 is startling: "Without faith it is *impossible* to please God." The professing follower of Christ must believe that God is! If you truly believe that God is, that He exists, then you must understand that He is immutable; He does not . . . cannot change. "Every good gift and every perfect gift is from above, and comes down from the Father of lights, with whom there is no variation or shadow of turning" (James 1:17). Faith comes by hearing and hearing by the Word of God! We cannot begin to serve the Lord without faith. It just isn't possible.

Why is it impossible? Because the work God has given to us on this earth as Spirit-filled believers is absolutely *impossible* by our own efforts. The only way we can fulfill God's mandate is through the supernatural. Isn't that what Zechariah made very clear? "This is the word of the Lord to Zerubbabel: 'Not by might nor by power, but by My Spirit,' says the Lord of hosts" (Zech. 4:6). What part of that don't we understand? Our abilities, our limited resources, our lack of experience have nothing to do with fulfillment of the Great Commission. Victorious conquest is always a matter of obedient faith and constantly drawing from the saving life of Christ who resides within us. (We'll discuss more about life-changing faith later in this book.)

Our Faith Promise Miracle

That Sunday morning in our little church, Dr. Smith challenged us again from the Word. We spent time in prayer, then distributed the faith-promise cards. The words on the cards are challenging: "As God enables me . . ." It doesn't say "my savings," "my bank account," or "my investments," but "as God enables me." I remember Smith's admonition as we prepared to fill out the cards: "If you have written a figure on that card, and you feel very good about it, in all probability God had nothing to do with it! For what God tells you to believe for will doubtless keep you up all night tonight!"

Could we really believe God for $20,000? Could we finally begin saying yes to missionaries who contacted us for funds? In the past we had said no to them because we had "nothing." But Smith had helped us to understand that we had exactly what we needed: *nothing* mixed with unshakeable faith. We had plenty of God's raw material—*nothing*!

We collected the faith-promise cards and tabulated the amounts. We waited for the announcement. You could have cut the tension with a knife. How strong was our faith? Had this whole week been nothing more than ecclesiastical hoopla? Had it been a mere motivational exercise? Or was there really something to God's call on our lives? The answer was exhilarating! The church treasurer stood behind the pulpit and with shaking voice reported, "The faith promise total for this coming calendar year is—$32,000!"

The place exploded! Please remember this was decades ago—$32,000 was an astounding figure from a small congregation that previously couldn't come up with $300 a week for its general fund! The announced faith-promise goal had been $20,000, which all of us "knew" was impossible. Yet the total of all the faith promises wasn't $20,000 but $32,000! What a wave of rejoicing swept through the church. Faith is liberating! Faith is exciting! Faith is rewarding!

Now we began to see the supernatural at work. There was no other explanation for the events of the next weeks. First, the tithing doubled within a couple of months! Instead of $200 weekly, it was $400 weekly. Within six months, it had doubled again. Every bill was cleared. We purchased a property just behind the church for desperately-needed office space. No, we didn't borrow the money; it was there—in cash.

Word spread, and the crowds began to come. Within one year, our congregation vaulted from 90 each Sunday to over 250. We had to rent properties nearby for Sunday school rooms. The youth met in a downtown nightclub we converted to a house of God. We began to say yes to any and all of our fellowship's missionaries. It was explosive! We were on fire. On Sunday nights our church was filled to capacity and often beyond capacity. It became "the place to be." And the funds just kept rolling in.

Isn't this what Jesus said would happen? "And He said unto them, 'Go into all the world and preach the gospel to every creature. He who believes and is baptized will be saved; but he who does not believe will be condemned. And these signs will follow those who believe . . .'" (Mark 16:15–17). He said that signs would follow those who fulfilled His commission to take the gospel to the whole world. Nothing on our part had really changed at the church; but now God had come in and taken control. There was simply no explanation for what happened except the supernatural. It was as if we were living in the book of Acts. We

were actually being "blessed!"

People were constantly being saved. Some of our choice people were called into the mission field. One of our most prominent couples (he was a well-paid pharmacist consultant) was called to missions and for the next thirty years served in Eastern Europe with Campus Crusade. We saw people healed; folks began to believe that God could do anything. Yes, yes, yes—signs and wonders . . . just as Jesus promised would happen. But note from Mark 16:16 that the signs *follow* obedience to the Great Commission; they never precede it. So often I've heard church leaders say, "When we get this building paid off" or "When we get an emergency fund for local needs" we'll support missions. But the blessings they want don't materialize before obedience, only after. They follow!

In the following months, other churches asked me to share the astounding story of our missions convention. Some congregations responded in positive faith and experienced results similar to those we had experienced. Other congregations wrote off the challenge as a fad and never followed through. Or they listened to a negative lament from someone. How sad that they listened to a naysayer instead of God's Word! Some folks told me I was crazy, that I was trying to hoodwink people into believing my "fairy tales." Ah, but we weren't experiencing fiction; we were experiencing God's supernatural supply.

As wonderful as that Sandusky experience was, it paled in comparison to what I would witness in the years that followed. Let me continue this amazing story of God's call.

CHAPTER ✿ SIX

AND THE BEAT GOES ON!

Four and a half decades have come and gone since that dramatic missionary convention of 1968 in snowbound Ohio. I rejoice to report that the mission-giving breakthrough wasn't a one-time happening. Indeed, I've witnessed the same type of victory again and again in churches cross-denominationally across the United States and Canada.

Someone on our staff did some research and informed me that around $250 million has been raised for global evangelization in conventions, banquets, and special events as a result of God's dealing with us in the Sandusky church. I've shared about that miracle in Pentecostal churches, Baptist churches, independent churches—congregations of many different persuasions. In all those experiences, I've never seen a church fail to reach its missions goal and, in most cases, exceed it two and three times or more. Not only have there been financial breakthroughs but spiritual victories as well (which must precede the fund giving).

That $250 million figure seems exaggerated and preposterous, but let me explain how so much of it happened.

About thirty years ago, I had the privilege of presenting this story of "Why Some Churches Are Blessed" at a three-day meeting of all the Assemblies of God churches in one state. At the close of the service, the state missions director asked if I would allow him to send out cassettes (remember them?) of my presentation to each of the over 400 pastors in that district. He also wanted to know what kind of royalty I wanted. I assured him that he was more than welcome to distribute the tapes to any and all persons, and I wanted no financial reward whatsoever. "Freely you have received, freely give" (Matt. 10:8). So the tapes were sent . . . and that's when the fun began.

I started receiving inquiries from pastors who had heard the tape. They wanted to share the presentation with their churches. I was thrilled! Then the tapes were sent across state lines, and I received letters from church officials and pastors across the country asking to duplicate the material. That I know of to date, tens of thousands of those cassettes have circulated around the U.S., not only in my church fellowship but in others as well.

The pastor of one church in Oklahoma called me to say that he plays the tape for his entire congregation every year—and has for almost ten years. The church had been giving a couple hundred thousand dollars to missions annually, but now the figure is over a million dollars. Praise God! I've heard similar testimonies from many other pastors. Faith is contagious! Ah, but so is pessimism and defeat. Sadly it's often easier to accept the negative report, as did Israel in Numbers 13. Two of the twelve spies sent to gather secret information in the Promised Land came back with glowing reports, but ten spies brought back the negative majority report and, as a result, the people refused to go into the land. They missed the reward that day because they chose to listen to the pessimists rather than trust God along with the optimists.

Now let me tell you a truly miraculously bizarre story, one that I'm still experiencing.

God Is Smarter Than We Are

Some years after pastoring in Ohio, the leaders of my fellowship asked me to head up the radio-television department in Springfield, Missouri. I felt God give His okay to this move. After one year, the fabulous C. M. Ward, speaker for the Assemblies of God international radio program *Revivaltime,* retired. To my shock, the leaders of our fellowship asked me to follow Ward. Notice I said "follow" him for no one could "replace him."

I loved that radio ministry dearly. We were heard on some 600 radio stations in 80 nations every week. I wrote 17 published sermon books, over 150 thirty-two-page booklets, and released a major series of recordings for children. A ministry of that magnitude needs an agency to represent it in the media, and we were taken care of by the Walter Bennett Agency in Philadelphia, in particular by their marvelous representative Robert Stratton. Bob also served Billy Graham and *The Hour of Decision.*

During the nearly seventeen years I had the joy of preaching on that broadcast, we received over 1.25 million letters from listeners all over the world. What an opportunity to spread the gospel! When the broadcast ended in 1995, *Revivaltime* was still rated number four in all Christian broadcasting by Dr. Brandt Gustafson, president of the National Religious Broadcasters.

As much as I loved the radio ministry, I wanted to pastor as well. I knew of some other national media preachers who served as full-time pastors, which I always felt added stability to their ministry. I loved one church in particular, located in the mid-central United States. The pastor there and I were good friends, and he scheduled me to speak there every six months or so. Over 2,500 worshipers gathered there every Sunday morning. In my personal prayers I often asked the Lord, "If that pastor ever leaves, please have the church call me to their pulpit. I would so love to pastor that great congregation."

In 1985, I had the privilege of speaking at the United States Military Retreat held in Berchtesgaden, Germany, at the famous General Walker Hotel. Upon arriving back in the U.S., a man from that church met me at the airport to inform me that the pastor had resigned, the church was open, and the board wanted to speak to me. I almost shouted, "Hallelujah!" But as I prayed about it, I felt that my prayers got no higher than the chandelier. The heavens had become that proverbial brass. I felt the Holy Spirit say to me, *"If you go to that city, you're on your own! I'm not going with you."*

I quickly informed the board that I wasn't interested in the position because I'm never going where God doesn't lead me. But, oh, I wanted to go. Why would the Lord not allow it? "'For My thoughts are not your thoughts, nor are your ways My ways,' says the Lord. 'For as the heavens are higher than the earth, so are My ways higher than your ways, and My thoughts than your thoughts" (Isa. 55:8–9). It often comes as a shock to us that God is smarter than we are. Imagine that! I understood those two verses in Isaiah and firmly believed them, but what could be higher or better than going to that exciting church as the pastor? I was soon to find out.

In the fall of 1986 I was home one Monday night watching a football game (that's what I do on Monday nights in the fall). The phone rang. My caller said, "Reverend Betzer, I'm calling on behalf of the church pulpit committee of First Assembly of God in Fort Myers, Florida. We are without a pastor and feel led to contact you. Would you prayerfully consider talking to us?"

I was grateful for the request, but I certainly didn't want to go there. The church had a reputation of a troubled congregation. Sunday attendance was once well over 1,400, but now it was hundreds less. There were huge issues that contributed to the attendance losses. Some, I had heard, were doctrinal. "Wolves" had gotten into the flock and consumed quite a few of the "sheep." In addition, the church was several million dollars in debt, and the financial institution that held the note was getting ready to call it in. I was fifty years old when I received that Monday night call and was looking for a church that was strong, financially well-off, and packed in attendance—not a broken one. I responded to my caller, "Thank you, but I don't believe I would be interested," and went back to watching the football game.

Several nights later, the gentleman called me again. "Brother Betzer, we believe God has put you on our hearts. Would you reconsider?" This time Darlene and I talked it over, prayed a little (not much because I didn't want to go to Fort Myers), and decided we owed it to that pulpit committee to at least fly down to confer with them, which we did.

It was a delightful group of about a dozen or so godly folks, both men and women, who served on that search committee. We talked for several hours. The committee spokespersons gave as accurate a report of their need as they knew it. As I listened, I was extremely negative in my spirit because I believed that the leadership needed there was far beyond any capabilities I might offer. And, besides, I was looking for a church, not an "opportunity." As the meeting ended, I said, "Folks, you've been wonderful to Darlene and me, but I don't feel that we should come to this church. Thank you, but no thank you." And the next day we flew home to Springfield.

Several days passed and I received another phone call, this one from Charles Petroskey. What a saint! For thirty-seven years he and his wife, Francis, had served as missionaries in Africa. Now in his later years, Charles was the visitation pastor of the Fort Myers congregation. He didn't hear well, so he talked quite loudly. When I answered the phone, I heard this thunderous, "Brother Betzer, this is Charles Petroskey. I just heard you turned down the pulpit committee. Is that right?"

I rather sheepishly replied that, yes, it was. Now came the scathing indictment: "Well, Brother Betzer, we've prayed about this and we know the mind of God. You apparently haven't prayed a lick about it! You ought to do so!" And, bam, he hung up.

Well, he was right about that. I hadn't prayed much about it because I didn't want to go. I would have to hear from God! I informed Darlene that I was going to a room to pray, and I wouldn't come out until God spoke to me in such a way that it was undeniable. It's a good thing I waited upon His voice to my heart; otherwise, as developments in the church took place in the next year, I would have left on the first plane out! It's essential that we know the mind of God in our service for Him. At 3 o'clock in the morning, the Holy Spirit said to me, "*Dan, I've called you to the church in Fort Myers. You go. Love those people. Do what I*

> **It's essential that we know the mind of God in our service for Him.**

tell you. And, Dan, don't blow it!" I kid you not, that was exactly the Lord's closing line: *"Don't blow it."*

We returned to Fort Myers on the Sunday before Christmas in December, 1986. I preached in both the morning and evening services, and Darlene and I went back to the office area as the congregation voted. The vote was 94 percent positive to call me as the pastor. The district superintendent who supervised the election called my family and me to the front of the church as he announced the vote results. Then he placed us by the communion table where people could come by and greet us. Their words were amazing. So many said, "Oh, we've prayed that this would happen." And "Thank the Lord you are coming." It was enough to make a person's head swell—for a little bit anyway.

Within the next year, about 400 of those people left the church! One business man from the congregation took me to lunch where he informed me that I was the "lousiest" pastor he had ever known. I was left with a remnant of folks (God bless those who remained faithful to the church!), the problems remained, and the debt was still there. Yet I felt reassurance that God was in it all. But my faith would be sorely tested in the next few months.

Witches, Bullets, and an Explosion

One morning shortly after assuming the pastorate, a young fellow entered my church study to talk to me. Very curtly he began, "We don't want you here." I replied, "Who is 'we'?" He informed me, "Within a circle of several miles circumference all around this church there are twelve covens of witches. We hate God, we hate churches, and we hate you. If you don't leave here, we plan to kill you." He let me know that he himself was a warlock, a male witch.

Within a few weeks, another young warlock came to our home in the dead of night while my family was sleeping. I was away in Iowa at a *Revivaltime* world prayer meeting. The fellow ran a long fuse from our street, across our yard, into the gas tank of my car, which I had filled with twenty-five gallons of high-test gasoline just the previous day. He lit the fuse and ran. The car was parked right next to our front door, and his goal was to blow up the car, believing the fire would expand, burn down our home, and kill everyone in our family. Fortunately he didn't know much about explosives. He surrounded the hose with rags, which disallowed any oxygen to mix with the fuel. So the car only had a small explosion, but it did set the car (which I loved) on fire. I got a call from Darlene informing me of the event. She called the police, and the incident went on the blotter as "attempted murder."

A few weeks later, the first fellow who threatened me in my office was saved, and I had the joy of baptizing him in water. When he emerged from it, he shouted for all to hear, "Satan, you lose!" But it was quite a few years later when a gentleman came to see me. He was about twenty-five years of age. We chatted some, and then he began to cry. I asked why the tears and he responded, "I'm the fellow who blew up your car and tried to kill you. Go ahead and call the police, and let's end this for everybody."

I told him that no police would be called, but that he and I would pray together. He said, "Sir, I will buy you a new car." I responded that I didn't want a new car (what was I thinking?), that God had forgiven him and I had too. I asked him why he put the fuse in my car gas tank and he said because the covens wanted me dead. Today that fellow is a pastor in a growing Nazarene church. Since that awful time, the covens have disappeared. Oh, the power of the cross of Jesus!

I couldn't understand why there was such animosity toward me and my family. Darlene came out of the shopping center one day to find her car covered with spittle and a note under the windshield wiper, "Go back to Missouri!" I received death threats by phone. Several nights the windows in the church were shot out. On another occasion people broke into my study during the night and trashed it.

Every morning as I woke up, I would pray, "God, get me out of here. I can't take this any longer." Out of the clear blue sky one day I received a call from a huge church up north. I was asked to consider pastoring that church—several thousand strong, all facilities paid for, no problems, no blown-up cars, no spittle, no threats. I breathed a prayer of thanks to God for getting me out of Fort Myers. But God spoke to my heart, *"Listen, Dan, I didn't call you there, I called you to be right where you are. And if you go to that other church you're on your own!"* Needless to say, I didn't respond affirmatively to that pulpit committee. I'm not going anywhere to attempt anything without the approval and the power of the Holy Spirit!

For a number of years, the great author and revivalist Leonard Ravenhill had been my mentor and like a father to me. What superb books he left us such as *Why Revival Tarries* and *Sodom Had No Bible* and others as well. Darlene and I often visited his home in Texas to experience a few days of guidance from both him and his precious wife, Martha. In my despair over what was happening in Fort Myers, I wrote to Leonard complaining about the car, the death threats, the window shootings, the spittle over Darlene's car, and all our woes. I frankly wanted some sympathy from the man I admired so much. But instead, here is what he wrote back:

> *Dear Dan—poor Dan, quite possibly nobody in the history of Christianity has ever suffered as much as you have. Martha and I were just discussing you this morning at breakfast, about what a privilege it is for us to know a martyr of your stature. Now—don't ever write a letter like that to me again!*

That's what you call a kick in the spiritual britches! Thank God for it. It drove me to prayer again. "Lord, what do we do? Help me!" It seemed that God patiently explained to me again: *"Dan, you are such a slow learner! Number 1, have a missions convention…"* Yes, it was the same information He had told me all those long years ago in Sandusky, sans Dr. Smith who had long since gone to be with Jesus. How quickly we forget! I must admit that all the badgering, the financial pressures, the opposition, and all those people leaving the church had made me temporarily lose my way. As the old saying reminds us, "It's hard to remember we were just draining the swamp when we're up to our necks in alligators!"

Our struggling congregation had put aside much thought about reaching people around the world. We were just trying to stay afloat. The prior year the missions giving was only a few hundred dollars weekly. But once again we determined to obey the Lord, impossible though His directives seemed, and, oh, the wonder of the results. An old hymn teaches us, *Trust and obey, for there's no other way to be happy in Jesus!*"[5]

CHAPTER 🌿 SEVEN

THE MOTOR OF THE CHURCH

A MISSIONS CONVENTION IS THE MOTOR OF THE CHURCH? That's right. For the past nearly twenty-eight years, the annual missions convention at our church has been the impetus behind every victory, every provision, every miracle. We advertise the convention with those very words: *the motor of the church.* Way back in Sandusky, at the original convention, God promised me that our conventions would never be dull. Further, that *motor* would drive the congregation for the coming year. God kept His word.

In order to obey the Lord in establishing a missions heart in the Fort Myers church, I asked a half dozen or so laity to meet with me as a missions committee. I believe so strongly in the lay people in the church. Somewhat facetiously I've told pastors in ministers' institutes, "Have faith in your laity! They're smarter than you. That's why they're not pastoring that church!" But seriously, I do believe in the laity; that's why our congregation is strongly laity-directed. It's amazing, really, how helpful and creative laity can be when given the opportunities.

I shared with the committee basically what I have given you so far in this book, how God had dealt with me back in the '60s. I taught them principles of faith-promise giving. We set the date for our first missions convention to be held the coming November, Sunday through Sunday. We discussed speakers, music, and various emphases.

Goals are vital for a missionary convention if you want to progress for Christ. I'm told that a fellow was driving through the countryside one beautiful day when he came upon a young man shooting arrows into targets on a barn. Every bullseye had an arrow dead center. The driver thought to himself, *I may be watching the greatest archer in the world! I'm going to stop and talk to him.* He approached the young man and said, "I've been sitting in my car, watching you shoot. You're incredible! What an archer you are! Why, you may be the best shot in this whole county!" The young man put down his bow, grinned, and replied, "Oh, I'm not so hot. I just shoot at the barn and wherever an arrow hits I paint a target around it." Perhaps a lot of churches do the same thing. If you don't aim at something, in any area of life, you'll never hit it.

In my heart, I prayed and hoped the missions committee would set a faith promise goal for that next calendar year of at least $100,000. That would be a huge increase over their previous year of giving for global evangelism—five times as much. I took a lot of time to teach them faith principles. I showed them Scripture after Scripture indicating that God would be our source. I finally said to them, "I want you to set the faith-promise goal for this next year. Whatever God lays on your hearts will be fine with me." And I left them to consider the proposition.

At the next meeting the committee members informed me that they had truly prayed and sought the Scriptures. They said they believed they had heard from God. I was on pins and needles for I was praying they would have mountain-moving faith for $100,000. And then they dropped the bomb! "Pastor," came the report, "we want to believe God this very first year for $175,000!" Hallelujah! Now that was a faith-promise goal! There was no way possible for our struggling church even to come close to it. Especially considering the financial institution holding our mortgage was ready to foreclose within a few months.

It was my job to break the news to the congregation, most of whom had no idea what was coming. Our sanctuary is a round structure, given to echoes from the sound distribution. Capable of seating several thousand, I remember preaching to crowds of 650 or so. I knew the echo would be there as I broke the news.

"Friends . . . ends . . . . ends . . . ends, God is directing us to hold our first missions convention . . . tion . . . tion . . . tion. We are going to hold it this coming November . . . er . . . er . . . er for eight full days . . . ays . . . ays . . . ays."

I could see people talking among themselves. "What did he say, Maude?" "Well, I believe he said we're going to have a missions convention, Henry." "A missions convention? What's he thinking about? Doesn't he know we're about to go into foreclosure here?" Oh, yes, I knew what they were saying. Did I ever!

I continued with the announcement. "And God has laid on our hearts a faith-promise goal . . . oal . . . oal . . . for this coming year of 175,000 dollars . . . ollars . . . ollars . . . ollars." As the echo faded away, I could read peoples' lips, "Is he crazy? We can't even meet our general fund budget! $175,000? That's impossible!" And I must faithfully report to you that some more folks left the church immediately.

The next week a businessman in the congregation asked me to meet him for lunch. It wasn't pleasant. "I'm leaving the church," he began, "for I can no longer accept your leadership. This mission convention thing is the last straw." And he added, "I don't know how you'll make it now for I'm pulling my tithe from the church. You may know, Pastor, that I give one hundred dollars every week." Only the restraint of the Holy Spirit kept me from laughing out loud. One hundred dollars? I could just see God on His celestial throne, clapping His hand to His forehead and moaning for listening angels to hear, "One hundred dollars a week? Oh, what will we do now?"

> **There it was again—the truth that Smith had drummed into me over and over: "Betzer, God will never owe you money!"**

The very next Sunday another businessman was saved at the altar. He, too, called me for lunch to ask, "Pastor, what is tithe?" I explained it to him, and he responded, "Excellent! My tithe will be $500 a week." There it was again—the truth that Smith had drummed into me over and over: "Betzer, God will never owe you money!"

I'll reserve an entire chapter later in this book to tell you about the missions convention and how God made it so vital and exciting. But let me give you the bottom line: On the last Sunday morning, after the tithes and offerings had been received as normal, I preached a message on faith-promise giving. We passed out faith-promise cards to everyone present, yes, even children and teens for I fervently believe they should be taught missions early in life. We read the cards out loud together: "As God enables me, I make a faith promise for missions for the coming year for $_____ to be given __ monthly, __ weekly, or in a one-time gift." Before praying and filling out the cards, I reminded the folks, "If you write something down on this card, and you're really comfortable with it, God probably didn't have anything to do with it. What God tells you to write will probably keep you up most of the night!" Then there was a place to sign their names.

For years we've burned the cards the day after the convention. No individual commitments are ever written down in the church records. Remember, the card reads, "As God enables me." Smith had taught me that no one would ever be reminded of the faith promise and no effort would ever be made to collect it. So why sign personal names if no record is kept and the cards are destroyed? I'll tell you why: When you fill out a faith-promise card with the figure commitment that God has laid on your heart and you sign your name to it, this makes you pray and seek God for His enablement. You take ownership of the commitment. It does something amazing to a person's faith.

Let me just tell you that the faith-promise commitment the last morning was well over $200,000! The actual missions receipts the following year were in excess of $257,000. I will explain how that happened a bit later in this book. The windows of heaven had been opened! But what about the mortgage? What about the bills? I remembered what God had done in Sandusky following our first missions convention. His supply had been supernatural, miraculous! But I was totally unprepared for what was about to happen next at our church in Fort Myers!

CHAPTER  EIGHT

SIGNS AND WONDERS

THE RESULTS OF THAT FIRST MISSIONS CONVENTION STUNNED US ALL. Money for global evangelism began to pour in. The pessimism that had infected so many about earlier church difficulties and the financial situation began to dissipate. General fund giving increased, but the mortgage we could not pay still hung over us like the dead albatross on Samuel Coleridge's Ancient Mariner. I had no ready answers for the people other than just hang on to what God promised in His Word. "But seek first the kingdom of God and His righteousness, and all these things shall be added to you" (Matt. 6:33).

I was convinced in my own spirit that the congregation was valiantly pursuing that reality. We were putting God first and global evangelism had become our priority. But where was the divine financial fruit? Our possibility of meeting a several million dollar mortgage within a few months was out of the question. I had to admit that I wondered how the congregation would be affected if worse came to worse and our church note was called and we lost our facilities, which consisted of some good buildings on thirty acres of land (on perhaps the prime corner location in town at that time). Would the people stare at me with disappointment? Would someone say, "All right, Pastor, we followed your leadership in the faith promises. How come we're losing our facilities? Where is God in all of this?" Sometimes, in the late night hours, I wondered the same thing myself.

We couldn't borrow the needed funds; our equity was too

small. Even if we could have borrowed the money, interest rates for that size loan in those days were in excess of 20 percent. One quote was given to us of 23 percent. Can you even imagine how quickly that monthly payment would have destroyed the church?

A month or so following the missions convention, I received a call from a gentleman I didn't know. He invited me to have lunch with him. Loving to eat and greatly appreciating Leviticus 3:16, which assures me that "all the fat is the LORD's," I joyfully accepted his invitation. He drove me to a local eatery that closed a short while later, which I regret because someone should have made a monument out of it. Why? Because that very day a spiritually-monumental event took place in one of those booths.

After a bit of small talk, the fellow, whom I will call Greg, leaned over his half-empty plate and said, "My wife and I are going to make First Assembly our church home." I was pleased to hear that and asked him why he had chosen us. His response was, "It's because you make missions around the world a priority. We've been looking for a congregation with that burden. We've attended a lot of churches that have great programs and pastors but the subject of missions is never mentioned."

He was right about that. First Assembly was all about missions at home and around the world. Indeed, emblazoned on both sides of the front of the sanctuary in every service are the three words that embody our philosophy of ministry: *reach, teach, send.* Everything we do has to fit into one of those categories. Within Christ's Great Commission is the command to go into all the world and *reach* the lost. Also within that edict we understand we are to *teach* the converts. And by the power of the mighty Holy Spirit we are to *send* forth laborers into the harvest. So my new friend and parishioner Greg had caught on quickly. Yes, he had observed correctly—our ministry was bound up in the Great Commission, then, now, and until Jesus returns.

Now the plot thickened. Greg leaned across the table and said to me, "I've just learned, however, that the church owes $100,000 on the gym. Is that true?"

I acknowledged that it was.

"Well," Greg hedged, "I don't want to belong to any church that owes $100,000 on a gym."

I conceded that it didn't make me happy either, but I had only been in town less than a year and the debt had been incurred prior to my arrival. I assured him that I was trying my best to get the debts paid. "And besides," I offered, "our big problem isn't just the gym but the sanctuary. We owe millions on it."

"Pastor," Greg said, "I'm not here to talk about the sanctuary debt. I'm here to talk about the debt on the gym." And he said it again, "I don't want to belong to a church that owes $100,000 on a gym."

By that time my old carnal, German nature was beginning to stir. I was about to say something I'm sure I would have regretted, when my host reached inside his coat pocket and took out a checkbook. He looked up and asked, "Do I make this check out to First Assembly of God?" I nodded that it would be fine to do that. I thought to myself, *Every fifty bucks or so will help us.* I about fell off the chair when Greg handed me a check for $100,000! I had never seen a check of that caliber before. (I've seen a bunch of them since—up to a million dollars!)

Greg looked me right in the eyes and asked, "Now, do you think you could go down to the bank and pay off that debt on the gym this afternoon?" I thought to myself, *Man, I can get there and pay it off before you can get to your parked car!* (Upon leaving the restaurant I rushed to the church, turned the check into our business office, called the church board members to report on the miracle, got a check from our treasurer to the bank, and was quickly on my way to "wash that mortgage right out of our hair!" Hallelujah! In one grand "Camelot" moment, the gym was paid for, freeing up a lot of desperately-needed money each month.)

Before I could leave the restaurant, Greg said to me, "Now, Pastor, let's talk about the loan on the sanctuary." He had my full attention. That debt was crushing us. Greg announced, "Pastor, I regret I can't *give* you the several million dollars you need on that sanctuary mortgage; however, I can *loan* it to you." I asked him in shock, "You have millions of dollars?" He replied, "Yes, I do. But I don't give it away. God has blessed me financially so I can help not only your church but others as well. Now here's the arrangement I'll make with the church. I will loan you the entire amount and charge you 8.5 percent interest. However, the church will make no payment to me of interest or principle for one full year. Instead, I will insist you use that interest payment to put together a ministry team. Do you think you could do that?"

> **Because we put God first and placed global evangelism on the front burner, God provided a supernatural supply.**

I almost choked on my dessert to think of 8.5 percent interest! Financial institutions were requiring twice that amount or more. I could hardly believe what Greg was proposing. "Yes," I finally managed, "I believe we could do that. I certainly need some staff!" Greg continued, "After one year, you'll start paying me the interest only. And we'll work together on getting the whole debt package eliminated as soon as God provides." Talk about a miracle! That morning had dawned with the overwhelming financial load burdening me almost beyond bearing. It was just another ordinary day of pressure and virtual hopelessness. Who would have believed the supernatural provision headed our way? Suddenly, out of nowhere, as Scriptures promise, God provided!

May I remind you that Greg and his wife joined our church because of missions! I'm convinced that had we not launched that initial missions convention, we might have lost the thirty-acre property and buildings. Truth be told, the church might not even exist now. But because we put God first and placed global evangelism on the front burner, God provided a supernatural supply.

More Miracles in the Making

God made it possible for us to pay off the entire note very quickly. We were debt free! But we needed other buildings. We had almost no Christian-education facilities. Our children were meeting in two large mobile buildings, which were not only unattractive but inadequate for reaching children with the gospel. Once again God provided, and not long after, we constructed a state-of-the-art children's center of over 50,000 square feet at a cost of $5.5 million dollars. We didn't have to borrow a penny on it as God provided every bit of the cost before we even opened the facility. To God goes all the glory and praise! We put Him and His kingdom first, and He began not only to supply the need but to provide additional supply. And all the time we kept adding missionaries. To date our church gives monthly support to 435 missionaries, and the list continues to grow.

As the congregation sought to put together a financial program that would allow us to build the children's center, the Lord put a fellow's name on my mind, an elderly somewhat-retired businessman. I felt led to contact him, show him the blueprint, and see if he would contribute toward the construction. I must admit that I argued with the Lord a bit, for this fellow, well into his eighties, wasn't a member of our church (and I'm not sure he had ever attended a service with us). But as I reasoned it out, I wondered if maybe the gentleman's heart might be touched by the concept of reaching children, and I asked the Lord to lay on his heart to give $50,000.

I had the faith for such a miracle, I believed, but faith without works is dead. I learned that the fellow lived on one of the top floors of a high-rise condo overlooking the nearby Gulf of Mexico. I made some calls and one of his employees reluctantly allowed me a short audience with the man in his home—a visit not to exceed fifteen minutes, I was told. When I rang the doorbell, an employee answered and invited me to enter. After a few minutes the old gentleman came into the room, saw the rolled-up blueprints under my arm, and snapped, "I don't belong to your church and have no funds to give." I quickly tried to explain what the Lord had put on my heart and prepared to leave. The man took the blueprints and said, "Well, I'll look these over and, if I have any interest, I'll call you. Don't call me."

I left with a heavy heart because I felt so clearly that God had told me to approach the man. The next day—yes, a very ordinary day, I thought—I got a phone call from the man himself. "Pastor Betzer, I want to invite you to have lunch with me in my condo. Can you come today? We need to talk about that proposed building." Could I have lunch with him? Does a hummingbird flap its wings really fast? Is LeBron James a great basketball player? "Yes, yes, I will be there."

This time, when I arrived, the man himself greeted me at the door and graciously ushered me into the dining room. A delightful lunch was ready for us, but first of all he wanted to talk about the children's center. Spreading our building blueprints over the table, he said, "Pastor Betzer, I've gone over these plans in great detail. What you propose with this structure to reach children for Christ is just incredible! This city has long needed such a facility. I want to participate in this project."

I thought to myself, *Well, glory! Oh, God, that $50,000 will be so helpful.* Try to imagine my shock when he said to me, "Now, pastor, I'm going to give money for this. You won't be allowed to use my name. I'm not doing this for any publicity whatsoever. Do you agree to that?" I nodded in the affirmative. "Good," my host said, "I'm going to give you one million dollars!" And he did! One million good old American dollars! When that amount was announced, it was like a cornucopia of divine supply opened wide to us and the money somehow poured in—all $5.5 million dollars.

For the most part, aside from that gentleman, the people at our church are ordinary people who have ordinary salaries, living from paycheck to paycheck. There simply isn't any rationale for what God has done here except the supernatural. And what triggered that supernatural? Missions! Our obedience to the Great Commission has allowed us to receive the blessings of God, not once, not twice, but over and over again through these intervening years. All glory goes to Him.

CHAPTER  NINE

A HOME-MISSIONS CHURCH
BUYS A BANK

A HIGHLY-PRODUCTIVE MISSIONARY TO A FOREIGN COUNTRY ASKED ME TO JOURNEY WITH HIM TO THAT LAND TO ADDRESS NATIVE PASTORS. I asked him, "What is the need there?" He responded quickly, "Faith! Teach about faith!" He continued, "Most of the pastors there operate only from what they can see or what they have at the moment. They seem incapable of believing God for what they don't have, and they need to fulfill their mission."

That lack wouldn't be confined to that nation alone; far from it. Nor would it be confined to pastors and church leaders. It's a malaise that seeps into the pew, into the thoughts of many followers of Christ. The absence of faith makes it difficult, no, impossible, to fulfill our mission; for the work God has given us to do is impossible with human strength and abilities. No matter how many other attributes we may have, individually or collectively as a congregation, if we aren't operating from the faith principle we can't please God: "Without faith it is impossible to please [God]" (Heb. 11:6). Let that word *impossible* resonate in your mind and heart!

I was blessed to be raised in an atmosphere of faith, believing for—and seeing—the impossible, both in our home and in our church. Let me tell you how it began.

In 1935, a twenty-year-old woman named Faye lay dying of cancer at St. Vincent's Hospital in Sioux City, Iowa. She was in a coma from which doctors assured her family she would never awaken. She weighed about sixty-five pounds.

A pastor was making his rounds through the hospital when the Holy Spirit led him into the cancer ward. The pastor observed Faye's desperate plight and walked to her bedside. There he took a small bottle of anointing oil from his pocket, gently touched it to Faye's forehead, and prayed a short prayer: "Lord, would you heal this woman?" That's it. No histrionics, no Hammond B-3 blasting out a rip-roaring song, no guitars strumming, just a simple prayer of faith! Faith! What does God's Word teach us? "Is anyone among you sick? Let him call for the elders of the church, and let them pray over him, anointing him with oil in the name of the Lord. And the prayer of faith will save the sick, and the Lord will raise him up. And if he has committed sins, he will be forgiven" (James 5:14–15). Pretty simple!

Then the preacher left the hospital and went home. Three days later . . . so did Faye! Yes, she walked out of the hospital and went home, discharged in good health. Healed! She lived another four decades or so of good health and vital ministry. I know this story well because Faye was my first cousin.

The pastor was Willis Smith. Pastor Smith was highly instrumental in the remarkable salvation of my father and mother. They were attending his little tabernacle-church by 1937 when I was born. Every sermon Smith preached imparted faith to his listeners. He pastored that small but growing congregation until early in the '40s when God called him to the Northwest. But he left behind a congregation with strong, yes, unshakeable faith in God. That was the atmosphere I breathed during those early formative years of my life.

There's an interesting sidebar to that story: Years passed and in 1963 my wife and I attended the Assemblies of God General Council in Memphis, Tennessee. One afternoon I was browsing through the exhibition hall when I spied Pastor Smith. I hadn't seen him since he had left Sioux City twenty years earlier, but I recognized him because of all the pictures of him my folks had kept through the years. I crossed the hall to meet him, put out my hand, and said, "Pastor Smith, I'm

Danny Betzer. You were my pastor when I was a child." A huge smile creased his face, and he boomed, "Oh, I remember you. You used to stand on a chair and sing in our services. And your father was a barber!" Well, that started a great conversation, and we had dinner together, reminiscing about halcyon years gone by. After the evening service, I walked Pastor Smith back to his hotel room. I hugged his neck and said, "You cannot know what an impact you and your messages of faith have had on me and my family!" He just smiled and said, "Thank the Lord, Danny. Let's have breakfast together." Then he went into his room. I was the last person to talk to him. Sometime during the night, while he slept, God took him home. He had breakfast with the heavenly hosts. Even on his last night on earth, his faith, his optimistic demeanor, his sense of hope, seemed to embrace his every word and action.

I can't thank the Lord enough that I grew up in a scriptural atmosphere of believing God for the impossible Why, every time I looked across the folks in our church, there would be Faye! How could anyone not believe in miracles?

Another Miracle in Sandusky

Now we race across the years to 1974 back to Sandusky, Ohio. God had called us back to the Lake Erie shores to begin yet another congregation. (The Holy Spirit seemed to have a penchant for cold weather because, once again, we began the endeavor in freezing temperatures, snow, and ice.)

We were meeting in the ballroom of a local hotel, situated at the causeway entrance to the famed amusement park, Cedar Point. The place was okay, but setting up a ballroom for church every weekend got wearisome. Some of us would arrive at dawn with trailers filled with chairs, a piano, an organ, Sunday school supplies, projectors—you name it. Plus we had to clean up the mess partygoers had left in the room from the Saturday night before. When our day's services were over, we had to reload everything back on those trailers and return them to storage until the next Sunday. We had only a few dozen people and no money. We knew we couldn't meet in that hotel for very long without losing whatever progress we had made. The age-old problem was we had no money and prices were outlandishly high everywhere along the Lake Erie shoreline. I prayed again and again, "Oh Lord, you see our need. We need a permanent home for this church. Help!"

Every Monday morning I took my payroll check downtown to deposit it at the Western Security Bank. How I loved that facility. Situated on the main downtown corner of town, it was a four-story marble structure that had been constructed in the '20s. The main room of the bank was just gorgeous. The walls and floor were made of Grecian marble. Some twenty-five feet above the floor, the ceiling was almost indescribable. Highly ornate with molded floral patterns, it was embellished with gold leaf. When illuminated by the two massive bronze chandeliers, the ceiling lit up in golden splendor, and about all you could say was "Wow!"

There was a mezzanine where the president of the bank had his office and another room nearby for his secretary. Above the mezzanine were two more full floors where some doctors and attorneys had their offices. Under the floor of the main room was a huge full basement. The building even boasted a historic elevator that still worked, operated by a lovely welcoming lady. Even the tellers' booths were made of marble. It

When God tells me something, I believe it. I just take it at face value.

was an amazing 27,000 square feet of marble, gold, and brass. Upon entering the bank I always felt that it was akin to being in a European cathedral. Well, maybe not exactly, but close. The Western Security Bank was just gorgeous, a landmark! I know the very sight of the building perked me up each Monday morning.

On this particular day, I was waiting my turn at one of the tellers' booths and praying. "Oh, Lord, you know our need. We so desperately need a building. Please help us, Jesus . . . please help us."

All of a sudden, standing right there in line, the Lord spoke to my heart with these exact words: *"I know you need a facility. And I'm going to provide you with one. In fact, Dan, you're standing in that facility at this very moment! This bank will the home of Calvary Temple!"*

When God tells me something, I believe it. I just take it at face value. God said that bank was going to be ours, and I accepted the reality of it. I was so moved in my spirit, even as I stood in that teller's line, that I began to cry. I seldom weep, but how could I help it? When I finally stepped up to the teller's window, the lady saw tears on my cheeks and said, "Pastor Betzer, are you alright?" And I responded that I was, but I wanted to say to her, "Get out of our building!" (Thank God for the restraint of the Holy Spirit!)

After she cashed my check, I went outside to walk through the two-square-block gardens that surrounded the bank. Every flower native to that part of Ohio was skillfully and carefully tended by the town's government workers. I tried to take it all in—massive trees, a huge clock made of flowers (the date on it changed every day with fresh arrangements), floral gardens in profusion, the big county office building with its tall clock tower, the city library building that looked like the home of some feudal lord, Sandusky Bay just down at the end of the street, and smack in the middle of it all was the marble building that God said was going to be our church home! I could hardly take it all in. To think that God was going to make such a place available to us! I had been praying for a building, any building, but my, my, my, not something like this! As David once wrote, "Such knowledge [was] too wonderful for me" (Ps. 139:6)!

In my many studies on the life of Joseph in the book of Genesis, I had learned vital lessons. Among them, this: Be very careful with whom you share your dream! I told no one of my encounter with the Lord in the bank that morning except my wife, Darlene. After all, who would even believe such a thing? I would be met by scoffing. "You must be dreaming, Pastor! That's impossible!" And how messed up such a thing could get if it were passed from person to person ("Have you heard what our young pastor is claiming? He claims our little church is going to get the historic downtown bank building on the corner! That he heard from God while standing in front of the teller's booth! Have you ever heard such nonsense in your whole life?"). No, like Mary, I just pondered that private experience with God in my heart, as did Darlene.

A month or so later, I picked up our local newspaper, the *Sandusky Register*, from our driveway. On the front page of the local section I saw a picture of the bank with this heading: "Historic Bank to Be Sold." The board of the bank wanted to build a facility that allowed "drive-in" banking, which the historic building couldn't accommodate. The building was going to be sold! Now was the time to go into action—all based on faith.

I convened the church board and told them the story. "Gentlemen, God is going to provide for us! The Western Security Bank is going to be our church home!" To their eternal credit, no one scoffed. But one of the men asked a terrific question, "Pastor, just how does a home-missions church with no money buy a bank?" I had no idea. Then one of the men said, "We should find out what the property is worth."

A fact-finding visit across the park to the county courthouse revealed that the bank building was tax-assessed at $6.5 million. We didn't have $650. Under normal circumstances the dream would have been crushed then and there. But in a continuing atmosphere of faith, the impossible seemed reasonable. So how much could we afford?

After a time of prayer and seeking the Scriptures, one of the board members suggested, "The figure that comes to me is $200,000. I believe we should meet with the bank president and offer to purchase that facility for $200,000." On several fronts his suggestion seemed ridiculous. What bank board member in his right mind would sell a tax-assessed $6.5 million building for $200,000? And second: We didn't have the $200,000. So I pointed to two of the board members and said, "Please make an appointment with the bank president and tell him that we're making a bona fide offer to purchase that facility for $200,000." One of the fellows looked back at me and said, "Hey, pastor, this is *your* dream! You're the one who heard from God, so *you* should make the offer." I asked one of the men to join me, and the following Monday we made the trek to the bank president's office.

As we rode the elevator to the mezzanine, every doubt in the world tried to shoot me down. But . . . I had heard from God! No question about it! We entered the president's office, and my eyes opened in wonder. It was a large room, about twenty by thirty feet. It was paneled, not in veneer, but heavy black oak slabs. The ceiling, twelve feet overhead, was held in place by massive, hand-hewn, split oak beams. On one wall was a huge stone fireplace with carved lions' heads on either side. I couldn't help thinking to myself, "Wow, what a study this will make!"

We sat by the president's desk, kindly accepted the coffee offered, and heard the man say, "So, gentlemen, what can I do for you?" Remember: I was the pastor of a tiny church, a *home-missions church* that not even a hundred people attended and we had no money at all. Still, I heard myself say, "Sir, we would like to purchase this facility." Now suddenly interested in us, the man said, "For what purpose?" And I responded, "For a church, sir."

He exploded. Pounding his desk, he thundered, "Do you really think we would sell you this historic building for another storefront church building?" The Holy Spirit now guided my response. "No, sir, I don't think you would do that. But I do believe you would allow this building to become a gorgeous cathedral where people can worship God!" His anger subsided and he leaned back in his chair. "Do you have any idea what it would cost you to obtain this building?" he asked. I braced myself, preparing for the worst because I was only authorized to offer $200,000. The president continued, "Gentleman, I'm going to give you one figure and one figure only. It has been set by the bank board of directors and it's non-negotiable. The cost of this bank building to you is $80,000!"

In shock, I muttered, "Wha . . . what did you say?" A bit louder he responded, "I said the cost is $80,000. It's non-negotiable. Take it—or leave it." I looked at my church board member who was staring right back at me. We were dumbfounded! What was the matter with that man? He was asking a little over $3 per foot for a 27,000-square-foot, marble, gold, and bronze building!

The bank president continued, "But there's a caveat!" My heart sank. What possible demand could he make of us? Had we come this far, been lifted so high, only to have all our hopes dashed? He informed us, "We would sell you this building for $80,000 only on the promise that you would never attempt to make this building a bank again! That will be a written part of the sale documents."

I wanted to laugh out loud! Hallelujah! I knew of far too many churches that considered themselves banking institutions, not supporting missions around the world but harboring a million or two dollars in banks as "slush funds" or "emergency funds." What is a greater emergency than millions of people heading for hell? I eagerly responded, "Sir, you have my word and that of all our folks at the church that we have no interest whatsoever in making this facility a bank ever again. It will be a center for worshiping God, for evangelizing, and for missions!"

The officer smiled, leaned back in his chair, and said, "Then, gentlemen, we have an agreement here. Let's start signing papers."

An hour or so later, my board member and I walked into the park surrounding the bank building. We couldn't believe what we had just experienced. A home-missions church with no money had just purchased a multi-million dollar facility for $80,000! But isn't that what God had promised? He had said He would provide a building for us. We had just had an excursion into the supernatural! Make no mistake about that! We had put God first, honoring the scriptural mandates for a Pentecostal church, and He had responded with a miracle. We were experiencing what Jesus promised, "Seek first the kingdom of God and His righteousness, and all these things shall be added to you" (Matt. 6:33).

The next week, we experienced a huge setback; one that required yet another miracle . . . or two.

CHAPTER TEN

"SO, WHAT DO YOU THINK ABOUT IT, MISTER MAYOR?"

GOD'S BLESSINGS OFTEN COME AT THE MOST UNEXPECTED TIMES, FROM THE MOST UNEXPECTED PLACES, AND IN THE MOST PRACTICAL OF WAYS.

The sales transaction to purchase the bank was done. What could possibly go wrong? Oh, lots of things. Among them was the task of getting the bank rezoned to be a church. What could be difficult with that? I mean, what could possibly go wrong?

The following Monday night I was at the Sandusky City council meeting. I had been there many times before in years past as the radio reporter for WLEC news and as a "stringer" for the Associated Press. I knew all the commissioners, the city manager, and the mayor. But on this night, years later, I was there as a supplicant, waiting for the opportunity to request the zoning change, flanked by the faithful church board members. The chamber was packed with interested citizens with their own agendas, as well as news media.

Near the end of the meeting, the mayor banged his gavel and asked, "Any new business?" That was my cue. I walked to the open microphone (the entire night was carried live on radio) and informed the commissioners that we, Calvary Temple, had just purchased the Western Security Bank and were requesting the zoning be changed to accommodate us. I honestly expected all-around smiles and the mayor to intone, "Why, of course, Pastor Betzer. We know you and are delighted to fill you request." Wrong! Instead I heard the mayor say, "Sir, do you have any idea how much property tax money comes into our coffers because of that bank? As a church you wouldn't pay property tax. Our city can't afford this, and I'm denying your request!" Bang! Down came the gavel and that was that.

The board members and I left the city building somewhat numb because of that callous rejection. One of the fellows said, "Pastor, we had better hire an attorney." I responded that I had already secured one. "Who is it?" he asked. "Jesus," I replied. "He's our attorney. He promised us the bank, and He'll take care of this!" And I went home.

I hadn't been there long before the telephone rang. The person calling was a reporter for the local paper, *The Sandusky Register*. She was their best reporter and was known for writing tough, noncomplimentary copy. She snapped at me, "I was at the council meeting tonight and heard that preposterous proposal you made. I couldn't believe what I was hearing. I'd like to interview you!" I replied, "Wonderful! When?" She said, "How about now? Can I come to your house tonight?" I replied, "Sure," and told her how to find us.

The reporter was a skinny little woman. My wife is a fabulous cook. When we got married in 1956, I weighed 140 pounds. Today I weigh . . . more. I asked Darlene if she could prepare a good meal for the reporter and she smiled and said, "Sure." So when the gal showed up at our doorstep I ushered her to the kitchen table and we fed her . . . and fed her.

Finally she opened her yellow pad, took out her pencil, and started firing questions at me. In earlier years I had been in the TV-radio news business long enough to know how to ask questions for which there is no good answer, that no matter what you reply, the questioner can take your responses and make you sound positively inane. That's the kind of questions I got from her. When she finished, she snapped shut her pad, got to her feet, and said, "Pastor, you won't believe what I'm going to write about you for tomorrow's paper." And she left.

It wasn't my fight; it was the Lord's.

Darlene asked, "What are you going to do?" I replied that I wasn't going to do anything. It wasn't my fight; it was the Lord's. He promised me the bank was going to become Calvary Temple. And I went to bed.

The next day the phone started ringing. "Pastor, get the paper!" "Pastor, have you seen the paper?" I picked up our copy from the driveway and opened it on the kitchen table. I could hardly believe what I was reading. That reporter had taken our side on the zoning issue! She wrote in glowing terms how our acquiring the bank could brighten the future of the downtown area. She even wrote some very nice things about me. As she read the article, Darlene asked, "Honey, are all those nice things she wrote about you really true?" I just smiled and answered, "Yes, of course."

The phone rang again and a deep voice came booming over the receiver, "Pastor Betzer, I'm the president of the Sandusky area chamber of commerce. I just read the story in today's *Register*. Can I come and see you now?" I told him to come on over and asked Darlene to fix a nice brunch. (I think this is why the Bible declares that we ministers are to be "given to hospitality.")

Into our house walked this tall, elegant man. He informed me that he and his friends were very unhappy about the mayor's and council's decision the night before. They wanted the zoning to be changed for us. I asked him, "What can I do?" He responded, "You can't do anything, but my friends and I can. Be at next Monday night's council meeting!"

All that week, the *Register* ran stories on our quest. Do you know how difficult it can be for a home-missions church to get any kind of publicity at all? Well, we were getting it every day, and on the radio as well as TV coverage. Remember the title on this book: *Why Some Churches Are Blessed*? We were putting God first and obeying the Great Commission. He was doing the rest, including providing us with an unbelievable building right downtown for $80,000! And publicizing our church across the whole county!

The next Monday night our board and I sat on the back row

of the city council meeting. The agenda was covered, and then the mayor asked, "Is there any old business?" My new friend, president of the chamber of commerce, stood, and you could feel electricity race though the crowded room. It was like the old western, *Gunfight at the O. K. Corral.* He said, "Mr. Mayor, I would like to introduce some of my friends, if I might. I would like all the members of the chamber of commerce to stand, please." About a dozen well-known people in town rose to their feet. "Remain standing," the president asked. "Now, Mr. Mayor, I would like the downtown merchants' association to stand please. Oh, my goodness, a whole group of business people stood to join with the chamber members. They, too, remained standing. "Now," continued the president, "could I ask all the downtown property owners association to stand and remain standing." By now, almost everyone in the room was standing. It was the "power crowd" of that whole area. The president said, "Mr. Mayor, all of us think that the bank should be rezoned in order to accommodate the request of Pastor Betzer and his board representing Calvary Temple. Mr. Mayor, what do you think?"

The mayor's face reddened, and he pulled the council members into a huddle. In a moment he said, "You know, sir, we, too, think it's a grand idea. We're going to rezone the bank immediately so Calvary Temple can take possession of that building and begin meeting in it immediately!"

Now, friend, *that's* a revival! I did nothing to make it happen. "To God be the glory! Great things He has done!"

I was already on that proverbial cloud nine as I left the council chamber when a gentleman approached me, "Sir, did your church really purchase that bank for $80,000?" I affirmed that we had done so. "Well, I own a downtown jewelry store. Would you be interested in selling that building to me? I will give you $750,000 for it tonight!" I told him that God had provided the facility for us and it was not for resale at any figure.

Another man, whom I knew, approached me as I walked to the parking lot. "Pastor, does the church have $80,000 to complete this transaction?" Honestly, that had never entered my mind. I said,

"Uh, no, we don't." To which he replied, "I'll have a check for $80,000 on your desk in the morning." And . . . he did exactly that.

"Signs and wonders," Jesus said "Seek first the kingdom of God . . . and all these things shall be added to you" (Matt. 6:33) . . . even a bank building.

CHAPTER  ELEVEN

STEPPING INTO THIN AIR

ON A RECENT VISIT TO MACAU, CHINA, I TOOK THE HIGH-SPEED ELEVATOR TO THE OBSERVATION DECK OF THE MACAU TOWER. The structure itself is nearly 1,100 feet high, but the observation deck wraps around it at 750-feet above the ground. The deck offers an unparalleled view of the Pearl River and, on a really clear day, Hong Kong, some forty miles away.

I raced out of the elevator to take in this panorama and shoot some exciting video, but I came to a screeching stop about halfway to the railing. Why? Well, I'll tell you why: the last twenty feet or so of the flooring of the deck, clear to the rail, is glass! Glass! Transparent—looking straight down through it—glass! There was a day in my life when that would have been the end of my "observing." I used to be petrified of heights. I was able to overcome it, at least to some extent, when I took flying lessons.

Here's what happened: On the first day of flight instruction, I climbed behind the yoke of a Piper Cherokee 140, scared half to death. My instructor, a brave fellow named Larry, climbed into the seat on my right, gave me some basic information, and helped me taxi the low-wing plane to the end of the runway. I know of few thrills to equal taking an airplane off the ground into the wild, blue yonder! Once airborne, Larry said, "Now, Dan, just keep pulling back on the wheel—the yoke—and let this plane climb." So I did. At about 10,000 feet, I felt the plane shuddering a bit and asked, "Shouldn't we be leveling off?"

To which Larry responded, "Climb!" The higher we flew, the more the plane shook. I cried out, "Larry, we're going to stall!" He answered, "We sure are!" And, sure enough, some 12,000 feet above the earth I watched the propeller stop, right there in front of my eyes, and we were in free fall. What was I doing? Screaming! It just seemed like the thing to do!

Larry quickly told me to knock off the histrionics and pay attention to his instructions. I did as he instructed, and the plane leveled off. I turned to him and demanded, "What was that all about?" He replied, "Dan, you can't learn to fly if you're afraid of the skies, the plane, or emergencies. You need to learn how to correct a falling plane." I somehow thought that lesson could have come a bit later! Like a year later!

So I remembered that first flying experience as I stepped out on the glass floor on the Macau deck. I kid you not—when you lift your feet off a cement floor and put it on a glass one, hundreds of feet up in the air, you think you're stepping out on *nothing!* The truth is that fitted glass is so thick an elephant could tromp on it, but your brain doesn't register that. My eyes saw the ground 750 feet down and told my brain, "You're gonna die!"

To me, practicing faith can sometimes be like that. If God has told you to do something, you're going to be all right, even though you're seemingly stepping into thin air. The precious Holy Spirit helps your brain assimilate His presence, and you trust Him—even when others might not. Yes, even catching the missions vision and acting upon it, although there isn't a farthing in the church bank account, can seem as if you're stepping into thin air. Perhaps that's one reason so many churches never take up the missions challenge.

> **If God has told you to do something, you're going to be all right, even though you're seemingly stepping into thin air.**

Faith and Obedience in Action

Let me share an early ministerial experience. In the late '50s I was hired to be the youth pastor of a church out east. In those days in our fellowship, the youth groups included those from thirteen to thirty-five years of age. How's that for a brilliant sociological grouping? I served in that position for two years and thoroughly enjoyed my first foray into ministry. I learned as I went along, and God truly blessed the youth group. I was having a good time!

One day the pastor called me into his office and said, "Danny, you're doing a fine job. Do you like it here?" I answered truthfully, "Yes, I really do." "So," he continued, "do you intend to stay on here?" "Yes!" I responded, "that's our plan, sir." To which the pastor said, "Then ... you're fired!" I was stunned. *Fired? Why? What had I done wrong? Hadn't he just told me I was doing a fine job? What was I to do now?* I had a wife and two small children to support. On a youth pastor's salary for the previous two years I hadn't been able to save any money. *Fired? How would my family survive this disaster?* I managed to sputter, "Why, sir? Why have you fired me?"

His answer was at least a little bit reassuring. "Danny, you have far more to do with your life than to stay here. I believe God has much more in store for you in the ministry." Then he softened the blow substantially when he added, "Now I want you to stay here for the next month. On your last Sunday, you'll preach in the morning service. We'll receive a love offering for you that will help sustain you for a while." There was a modicum of comfort in that, but how could I go home and tell Darlene I had just been fired? And what in the world would we do? Let me tell you, I was extremely limited in ministerial experience.

For example, I didn't know how to preach. I had only done so a half dozen times in my life, and those efforts were far from successful by anybody's standards. In fact, in my last effort, a lady in the audience went crazy, jumping on a pew and screaming, "You're all going to hell!" That slowed down my ministerial career enthusiasm!

When I got home, I told my wife the grim happenings of that day. Her response was fabulous! In about six decades of marriage, never once has that dear mate of mine discouraged me or disparaged my work. She and I earnestly prayed, seeking God's direction on what He wanted us to do. We felt the Lord leading us to an itinerant ministry. I must explain this: I'm not an evangelist. One of the ministry gifts

God has given the church, according to Ephesians 4:11–12 is that of the evangelist. A preacher who travels is not necessarily an evangelist. In my case, I was simply a "fired" former youth pastor trying to find places to let me learn to preach. Getting into some churches would be a sort of pulpit laboratory to assist me in that pursuit. I'll forever be grateful to pastors who helped me, who patiently bore my "often-borrowed" sermons and the ineptness with which I presented them. But . . . a person has to learn.

Both Darlene and I have always been musical. She's a gifted pianist and organist, and I've been singing since I was a kid, so that helped us. Miraculously, God enabled me to schedule some meetings around the country, most of them for a week. In all honesty, God did make it possible for some of those "revivals" to be eternally worthwhile. We saw quite a few people commit their lives to Christ during the altar services. In the second year, amazingly, invitations to churches large and small began to come frequently, allowing me to book the year 1963 completely, January right through December. I didn't have an open night for the entire year. We settled into that particular ministry, even purchasing a little better car, believing our traveling for the Lord would continue for some time.

Then I came to the "glass floor in the observation deck."

During the last ten days or so of December, 1962, Darlene, the kids, and I were with her parents for Christmas. The Lord was blessing our newly-explored ministry, and I found myself truly anticipating the traveling circuit in the coming year. For one thing, we were scheduled from New Year's through March in Florida . . . warm, wonderful Florida! How much better could it get?

In the meantime we enjoyed spending those days in the home of Darlene's folks. Christmas Day I was praying during the morning, and once again I felt God speak to my heart. I wasn't eager to receive this message! His challenge to me was this: *"Danny, your itinerant ministry is over as of now. Today I want you to contact every pastor with whom you are scheduled in the coming year and cancel the meetings. I have something else in store for you."*

I was shocked. Speechless! Darlene and I had worked so hard to build the itinerant ministry into something strong and viable. We gave of our best in every church, never asking for a dime, taking only the "love offerings" that were given. God had seemingly blessed the efforts, and we could anticipate the year ahead with confidence, knowing our small needs would be adequately met. I would have the joy of preaching in some pretty large churches, too, which was a new blessing. What a learning experience it would be for me, preaching to hundreds instead of dozens! And now . . . God wanted all that to go by the boards? To be arbitrarily canceled?

Darlene is my life's partner and we do things together, including planning our days, months, and years under God's direction. I told her what I felt the Lord had told me, that I was to cancel every meeting for the coming full year. She replied that she felt the same witness, that God had revealed to her as well that our days of traveling in such ministry were over. I asked her if she was comfortable with my canceling every meeting—every single one—or should I retain a few of the larger churches, just in case. After all we had to eat and live somewhere. She replied that she was sure God was leading us someway or other and she was comfortable with erasing the whole schedule. All of it!

In those days there was no email. We had "snail-mail" and the telephone. I couldn't afford to make many long distance phone calls except for those pastors who were expecting me in January. So my work was cut out for me to contact each of those good pastors to explain the cancellations. Every one of them was kind and gracious. (Perhaps they were relieved). They said they understood and prayed that God would bless our family and provide for us.

Christmas night wasn't an easy one of rest and sleep for me. We had perhaps enough money for two weeks of normal living. Then what? Where were we to go? What were we to do? What would I even tell Darlene's folks? The next morning I would learn again something I never should have forgotten: The glass floor is solid!

About mid-morning the phone rang, and Darlene's father

told me the call was for me, long distance. I thought it might be one of those pastors I had cancelled the day before, but it wasn't. It was the district superintendent from Ohio. I had never met the man and couldn't imagine what he would want with me.

He began, "Brother Betzer, I want to talk to you about an opportunity for ministry in Ohio." He said that the quaint town of Vermilion, nestled right against the southern shore of Lake Erie—halfway between Cleveland and Toledo—urgently needed an Assembly of God church. For years, the population there had been around two to three thousand. But recently Ford Motor Company had established a huge assembly plant right between Vermilion and Lorain, bringing in over 4,000 jobs. Suddenly Vermilion had become a boom town of around 10,000 people, a great many of them from West Virginia. The superintendent said, "Brother Betzer, would you be interested in praying about this opportunity and consider starting the church there? By the way, there's no money, no salary. You'll have to raise every dime and start from absolute scratch."

I felt the Lord confirm in my spirit, *"Dan, this is why I had you cancel all those meetings. I'm calling you and Darlene to Vermilion!"*

I responded to the superintendent, "Yes, sir, I would be wide open to this call. When do you want us there?" There was a pause and he said, "Well, don't you think you ought to pray about this?" I informed him of God speaking to my heart the day before about cancelling all those revival meetings and opening the way for an entirely different ministry. To which he responded, "Well, then, how soon can you get here?" I answered that we would be there by the first of the year—just a few days away.

Several days later, my family and I left for Vermilion, pulling behind us a U-Haul trailer containing everything we had in the world. We had received a few Christmas gifts of cash so we had close to a thousand dollars to our name—heading for a place we had never been, to minister to folks we had never met, and to do something we had never done. That, my friend, is a glass floor! Without faith it is *impossible* to please God!

A bit of additional information here: We pulled into Vermilion the first Saturday afternoon of January, 1963, in a blizzard. No offense to northerners, but I don't like snow. I don't even want to see pictures of it! I remembered asking God for a "beach ministry." But not the Lake Erie beach!

As we approached the town, I was praying even as I drove, "Lord, I have no idea what to do here. How do I start a church? Help me!" How faithful our Lord is to undergird our calling. On the screen of my brain, God revealed to me exactly what He wanted done and how we were to do it. Let me promise you that what God wanted required a whole lot of faith!

Eighteen months later we dedicated the beautiful new Vermilion Assembly of God church with over 250 people in attendance that night (although we averaged about 140 on normal Sundays). It was an amazing night! It came on the heels of miracle after miracle of God's provision. Fulfilling His call on our lives quite often causes us to feel that we are stepping into thin air! But, oh, dear friend, God is faithful! Always! So take that step! Step on the glass floor—into seemingly thin air!

CHAPTER  TWELVE

WHY EVEN BOTHER?

D URING THE SEVENTEEN YEARS I WAS THE PREACHER ON
THE *REVIVALTIME* RADIO NETWORK MINISTRY, I BELONGED
TO THE NATIONAL RELIGIOUS BROADCASTERS ASSOCIATION
(NRB). It was my privilege to serve on the board for over a decade. One
year, our radio team was invited to present the broadcast during the
annual convention in Washington D.C., which was held in the Hilton
Hotel near the White House. That's the hotel where President Reagan
was shot and nearly killed shortly after his election. Our broadcast was
the second feature of the night; the other was a message from one of
America's best-known television pastors.

He was a fine gentleman, warm and gracious. Backstage I
asked him to share with me some of his pastoral "secrets." He responded
that what he would tell me was not particularly a secret; however, it
became one of the most cherished bits of pastoral counsel I've ever
received. Further, it had never been explained to me so powerfully,
so practically.

He explained to me there are three things that every pastor
should know. (They are vitally helpful to laity as well.) They were in
the form of questions:

1. *What in the world are you trying to do?* That sounds like such
a fundamental query. Why, everyone knows what they're trying to
accomplish . . . . don't they? However, in my studies I've found that
precious few pastors or church leaders can answer that question.

George Barna, in his book *The Power of Vision*, reported that some polls have revealed that many leaders cannot clearly articulate what they are trying to do.[6] As for church leaders, if *they* don't know what they're trying to do, how can the people they serve know it? I've received such responses as, "Well, we're trying to reach our city for Christ" or "We're praying for a revival." While well-intentioned, those responses are nebulous. "What you're trying to do," explained my pastor friend at NRB, "is your *philosophy* of ministry." Everyone you serve should be able to articulate it precisely.

In the '70s I pioneered a church in Ohio. There was a pastor in our fellowship on the West Coast who had been enormously successful. I called his church secretary to make an appointment to spend several hours with him to pick his brain. I flew cross country at my own expense, rented a car, and showed up in his office. I thanked him for his time and said, "I just want you to give me wisdom on starting a church." He stared at me and said, "I'd like to see your written statement of what you're trying to do."

I stuttered, "Well, I don't have such a thing, sir." He responded, "Then go back home and when you have one come see me again." I had flown out there for nothing, I thought. But a month or so later I did return *with* a written statement of our philosophy of ministry. The pastor said to me, "If you don't know what you're trying to do well enough to have it written down, you're wasting your time." Then he proceeded to give me some terrific foundational information on reaching my town for Christ.

2. *How in the world do you propose to do it?* Do what? Fulfill your philosophy. That's *vision*. Proverbs 29:18 warns: "Where there is no vision, the people perish" (KJV). People die! What good is the *philosophy* if there is no plan (*vision*) anointed by God to make it happen? So a church leader may claim, "What are we trying to do? Why, reach our city for Christ!" Really? And exactly how do you plan to do that? What's your vision? The common response, often accompanied by blank stares, is, "Why, we're really praying about it!" My friend evangelist Reinhard Bonnke sat in my study one night and lamented, "Dan, we need to

pray . . . of course we do; but unless we put faith and action into our prayers—and vision—we're just treading water."

As a pastor for decades, I find myself constantly seeking God for the *plan*. I know what the Lord wants me to do. But how does it get done? Did God give us a brain for a reason other than just separating our ears? Or are we just casting in the dark? Scripture reminds me, "Dan, if you don't have vision—a plan—people are going to die and be lost for all eternity!" Now that's serious business. How desperately I need faith, without which I cannot please God! And I also must have the infilling of God's Holy Spirit for the enablement promised by Jesus in Acts 1:8. So what in the world am I trying to do? And how in the world do I plan to get it done?

3. *Why in the world do you even bother?* Simply put, what motivates me? What keeps me going? What drives me? Why don't I just give up when the going gets tough? For the answer to this question, I turn to Paul in his first letter to the Corinthians, and his lesson is really a shocker!

> For we are God's fellow workers; you are God's field, you are God's building. According to the grace of God which was given to me, as a wise master builder I have laid the foundation, and another builds on it. But let each one take heed how he builds on it. For no other foundation can anyone lay than that which is laid, which is Jesus Christ. Now if anyone builds on this foundation with gold, silver, precious stones, wood, hay, straw, each one's work will become clear; for the Day will declare it, because it will be revealed by fire; and the fire will test each one's work, of what sort it is. If anyone's work which he has built on it endures, he will receive a reward. If anyone's work is burned, he will suffer loss; but he himself will be saved, yet so as through fire. (1 Cor. 3:9–15)

There it is: the motivation! I must one day stand before the Lord and give an account for my obedience and stewardship since the day I was saved. It's one thing to be accountable to a church board, or a superintendent, or whoever, but to be accountable to Christ is a whole different ball game. We wax positively eloquent about the alleged rewards God is piling up for us in heaven. Well, we ought also to sing, *It Ain't Necessarily So!* There are no mansions promised to us. No double-decked bejeweled crowns. "Well, what about John 14:2? Jesus said we would have mansions." No, He didn't. He said there were many mansions there where He was going and then added, "I go to prepare to prepare a place for you." There's a huge difference between a mansion and a place! I should know for I've lived in a lot of places. So far—no mansions!

Scripture makes it clear that we can't earn salvation for it's the gift of God to those who believe. However, rewards must be earned! Look at 1 Corinthians 3:14: "If anyone's work which he has built on it endures, he will receive a reward." All the works we have accomplished on earth, allegedly for the Lord, are going to be tried by fire. By fire! So what if all our works are the hay, wood, and stubble Paul listed in 1 Corinthians 3:12? There will be a flash of flame and ashes, nothing left. So what are those highly combustible works? Anything we do on this earth for our own glory or credit are the hay, wood, and stubble.

When does this "audit" take place? "The day will declare it" (v. 13). What day? The judgment seat of Christ! This hearing will not be to determine whether we are saved or not, for we won't even be there if we aren't redeemed by the blood of the Lamb. Don't confuse this judgment with the great white throne of judgment that determines the fate of those who have rejected Christ. Well, what's this judgment seat of Christ for anyway? Why are we all there? We are headed for the marriage supper of the Lamb. The Lamb, of course, is Jesus Christ. We, the church, are the bride of Christ. Christ is the eternal groom. The marriage supper is for Him, not for us.

Years ago I made a film in Israel. The purpose was to film social mores extant in Jesus' day that probably are not still valid. Our Israeli host took us to a village where a wedding was taking place. The factor that made this wedding so unique and film-worthy was that it was being done as a wedding would have been conducted in Jesus' time. I wanted close-ups of the bride, but my team informed me they couldn't find a woman anywhere. The square was filled with celebrants, singing, dancing and eating . . . but . . . no bride. Everything was for the groom: the feasting, the music, and the gifts. When the wedding reception ended, the fellow went to his fiancee's home to whisk her away to a honeymoon somewhere. I was shocked! The entire marriage celebration was for the *groom!* Men, where have we dropped the ball on this? Today, in our culture, the bride is featured. If we think of the marriage supper of the Lamb in terms of weddings today, we miss the point. The marriage supper is for the Lamb, for the Holy Son. He is the eternal groom.

To make sure that we, the bride, don't go traipsing into this holy marriage supper with apparel or anything else that would take attention away from Jesus, we will have our "trousseaus" checked at the gate: the judgment seat of Christ. All the works we did for ourselves rather than for Christ will be burned up. Read it again: "If anyone's work which he has built on it endures [survives the test of fire], he will receive a reward." Gold, silver, and precious stones won't be destroyed by the flames. Those efforts of our earthly lives motivated by our passionate love for Jesus will not only survive the fire but will be refined, and our crowns and diadems will be fashioned from them. We will have these treasures to lay at the feet of Jesus at the marriage supper.

So, why do I even bother to serve Christ? What motivates me? It's the stark reality that I will one day stand before Him; saved, yes, but not necessarily with any gold, silver, and precious stones. I love to preach and teach. Why do I do it? Yes, I enjoy it, but do I minister to gratify my own flesh or to lift up the Master? Do I just enjoy standing in front of people and talking? As a matter of fact I do enjoy it, but is that why I do it? Why do choir members sing? Why do ushers do their needed work? Why do I tithe? Just to get a tax write-off? Or do I give because of my love for Jesus?

I often wonder how we will be called before the judgment seat. We know that God is a God of order, so there must be some fashion in which He will summon us. If, by some possibility, God called us before the judgment seat in alphabetical order, I'm most grateful I don't have a name beginning with the letter "P." I don't want to be anywhere near the apostle Paul when he stands before the reviewing stand. Let's try to imagine it:

A thundering voice from an archangel cries out, "Paul . . . apostle Paul, front and center!" All of us in the heavenly grandstand crane our necks to get a first look at this majestic missions champion. Leonard Ravenhill used to tell me he thought Paul might walk with a "holy swagger." I always imagined Paul walking like John Wayne. What a man! He once wrote that he had been beaten numerous times, that he had been shipwrecked three times, that he had gone without proper nourishment, that at one time nobody in Asia Minor (Turkey) would even speak to him, that he had been stoned and left for dead by the side of the road. But he also testified, "None of these things move me" (Acts 20:24). Wow! Paul never said those things didn't *hurt* him, only that they didn't *move* him.

Note carefully that Paul didn't dread this eternal audit before the Lord Jesus. On several occasions I've trembled from the chill in the bowels of the ancient Mamertine Prison in Rome where it is believed that Paul spent his last days prior to his beheading and where he wrote the book of Second Timothy, often referred to as his last will and testament. In his poignant letter to his young "son in the faith" Timothy, Paul wrote:

> I am already being poured out as a drink offering, and the time of my departure is at hand. I have fought the good fight, I have finished the race, I have kept the faith: Finally, there is laid up for me a crown of righteousness, which the Lord, the righteous Judge, will give to me at

that Day, and not to me only but to all who have loved His appearing. (2 Tim. 4:6–8)

What a line: "The time of my departure is at hand." Hey, soldiers were coming to cut off his head! What panache! What flair! Instead of moaning about his fate, Paul wrote as if he was about to board a jet for Paris, "The time of my departure is at hand!" He knew he was ready to appear before the Lord and to receive a crown of righteousness on "that day." What day? The judgment seat of Christ.

As Paul stands before the throne, we hear God ask, "Paul, what did you bring to me from your earthly sojourn?" One by one we see the first missionary bring his accumulated treasures from the field: the family of the Philippian jailor, Lydia (the seller of purple from Thyatira, Turkey,) the saints from the Greek cities of Berea and Thessalonica, some from Athens, the many believers in Corinth, Ephesus as well, . . . and the list goes on and on. Finally, when it appears that Paul has completed presenting his eternal hope chest to the Lord, God asks, "Is that it, Paul? Are you finished?" The grand apostle gazes upon the face of the One he loves best and responds, "No, no that's not all." We watch as Paul opens the collar of his tunic and with a finger traces a somewhat faded red scar that traverses 360 degrees around his neck. "See this scar, Lord? This is where the Roman axe went through my neck. You ask me what I bring to this audit? My life, Lord, my life! I gave you my life!"

Now, my friend, do you want to follow Paul at the judgment seat of Christ? Someone will, unless God in His mercy allows Paul to be the last one at the throne. I don't want to be anywhere near Paul on that auspicious day. God will then take all of Paul's treasures and try them by fire. And from the purified gold, silver, and precious stones will come Paul's eternal rewards, which he will then lay at the feet of Jesus.

Suppose all your labor on this earth has been for your own pleasure or benefit. That's all hay, wood, and stubble and will be burned to ashes by the fire. You will have nothing to lay at Jesus' feet but ashes. 103

While nearby, Paul kneels at the scarred feet of his Savior and lays the record of converts from around the world, eternal treasures he discovered at enormous sacrifice to himself.

So, in response to question number three, why do I even bother, I reply with this verse: "For we must all appear before the judgment seat of Christ, that each one may receive the things done in the body, according to what he has done, whether good or bad" (2 Cor. 5:10). That is why we bother!

CHAPTER ✿ THIRTEEN

PLAY BALL!

WHY ARE SOME CHURCHES BLESSED? Somehow the leaders and congregations of such churches see things as God sees them—at least for the moment. They act on what they see in their spirits. They set aside their limitations and doubts to rely on divine intervention. As a result, amazing things happen. All too often we sing *How Great Thou Art* on Sunday morning and then react to challenges on Monday as if God had died during the night. If God is great on Sunday, is He still not great on Monday?

Let me tell you a story from my personal life experiences. As I've mentioned before, in their field of ministry the men and women who serve on my staff are smarter than I am. Otherwise, why would I hire them? I not only hire these smart, anointed folks, but I give them the liberty to minister effectively. Some leaders won't do that for one reason or another. Fear perhaps? Insecurities? Remember when Jesus raised Lazarus from the dead, He commanded the onlookers to take the grave clothes off of him: "Loose him, and let him go" (John 11:44). Well, that's what I attempt to do with my staff.

A leader who keeps their thumb on everyone and everything isn't likely to get as much production from the staff until they are "loosed and let go." Nor are the staff members liable to stay with that leader for long. I'm blessed to have several of my staff who have been with me for over twenty years and one for nearly twenty-six years. I give them the liberty to unleash their enormous abilities and vision.

Yes, there's accountability, to be sure, but there's also the greatly needed freedom of talent and expression. Hank Peters, one of major league baseball's finest general managers, said, "I believe in delegation of authority! I don't believe in one-man shows." We pastors can learn a ton from that!

I remember clearly the first time 2,000 people attended our church on an Easter Sunday. What a celebration! I can also remember Sundays when we had about 600 in that big sanctuary. They looked like BBs in a boxcar. So, wow, 2,000 in church? Hallelujah! The day following Easter I met with our staff as I usually do on Mondays. We were rejoicing in the victories of the previous day when I blurted out, "Hey, gang, let's shoot for 5,000 in attendance next Easter!" The Bible teaches clearly that God isn't willing that anyone be lost, so there has to be a way to reach them. "Yay, Pastor, let's do it," was the general response, until one practical fellow asked, "Uh, where are we going to put 5,000 people in this church? Our sanctuary seats only 2,000." See, I've always believed that pastors are supposed to be the visionaries and their staffs are supposed to make it happen! Just kidding . . . sort of.

At that point, another staff member had the temerity to propose, "Say, Pastor, the Minnesota Twins ball team has just built a gorgeous spring-training stadium in town. It seats 7,500 fans. How about that for a site?" I'm delighted to work with the kind of people who didn't immediately respond, "What, are you crazy? A baseball stadium on Easter Sunday? Why, we won't have enough people to make the crowd look respectable. How could we even afford something like that?" Thank God, we don't have to work around knee-jerk reactions like that.

I responded, "Okay, let me get the Twins people on the phone line here." And while the whole staff watched, I got my secretary to put me through to one of the baseball executives.

Ring . . . ring . . . ring . . . (Did you ever call someone with an idea that was crazy and each time the phone rang you hoped no one would answer?) "Hello!" I actually got through to somebody. "Hello," I responded, "could I talk to someone in charge of leasing out the stadium please?" There was a short pause on the other end, which I figured happened because that person wasn't accustomed to such a request. "One moment, please."

Another click and a fellow's voice came over the line, "Hello, how can I help you?" I said, "This is Pastor Dan Betzer of First Assembly of God church here in Fort Myers. Yesterday we had several thousand people attend our church and next Easter we would like to have 5,000. We can't possibly seat that many in our sanctuary, and we're searching for an alternative venue. Your stadium has been suggested as a possible location. Can we talk about this? Is it possible to rent the stadium for a day or two?"

"Well, this is an unusual request, Reverend. How long would you need the facilities?" I answered, "Well, most of the day on Saturday for rehearsals and set-up and that night as well with the stadium lights on because we'll be building a huge stage over second base, setting up sound, TV cameras, and so forth. Then Sunday morning we will need it probably until early afternoon for the actual service. Oh, and we need a couple other practice diamonds so we can set up tents for children, counselors, and so forth."

There was another pause and my responder suggested, "Sir, that's a very ambitious program you have in mind, and we've never been asked to do such a thing in this new ballpark. So let me talk to our people here and I'll call you back. Let me get this straight now—you want the stadium all day Saturday and also that night with all the lights on. Right? Plus Sunday morning until early afternoon and a couple of the practice diamonds to erect tents. Do I have this right?"

"Yes, sir," I answered. My new friend (I hoped!) at the stadium said, "I'll have to call you back." "That's fine," I returned, "and my staff and I are sitting here in my office eager for your response." I hung up. Even as I talked to the fellow, my brain was attempting to tabulate how many thousands of dollars it would cost to rent that magnificent place (which had been built to remind people of Churchill Downs in Louisville, Kentucky).

The staff and I bowed our heads and asked God for a miracle. We had hardly finished praying when the guy from the ball team called me back. "Hello," I called out. What I heard next was incredible; in fact, only God could pull off something like this. "Well, Reverend, we're going to give you a positive response to your request. You can have the stadium for the times you asked about: all day Saturday, Saturday night with the ballpark lighted, and on Sunday until early afternoon. Now let's talk about the rent."

I gave the thumbs up to the staff who couldn't hear the other side of our conversation. Now . . . the big hurdle! The money! The baseball executive said, "Okay, here's the deal, we can let you have the stadium, and we'll ask you to pay us . . . $100." I couldn't believe what I was hearing. Why, we would burn up that much electricity that Saturday night on each pole in the outfield. "$100," I asked, "for the whole deal? For both days? Did I hear you right . . . $100?" "Yeah, that'll take care of it," he assured me. I then heard myself ask this executive, "Uh, sir, would you consider allowing us to rent the stadium every weekend?" With that kind of a deal, our church would have made a major move, I can tell you that! He laughed and said, "No, let's just settle for this one time, okay?" "Yes, sir," I answered and said, "I'll call you back later for some details. Thank you, thank you, thank you!" And we both hung up.

I turned to the staff and reported, "We just rented the Minnesota Twins spring training stadium for the whole weekend for a hundred bucks!" The room reverberated with "Thank you, God" and other praise expressions.

Then one practical fellow on staff asked, "Pastor, we have the stadium, and we have a couple thousand people who attended here yesterday. Thank God for the miracle of renting that place for only $100. That's great. Now . . . where are we going to get the rest of the people to fill that place?" Good question. See, you can't just dream and imagine that spectacular things are going to happen. Faith without works is as dead as a carp! "What does it profit, my brethren, if someone says he has faith but does not have works" (James 2:14)? Our staff discussed the eternal reason that we had to fill it: because hundreds of souls were at stake. We were not shooting for 5,000 people just to get a plaque or hear other church leaders say, "Ooooohhhh! Did you hear about First Assembly?" God forbid that such should be our motivation. No, this would be an evangelistic enterprise of the first dimension. We sincerely wanted to win a whole lot of people to Christ.

Do you know what happens when you push the "creativity button"? Ideas explode! Innovation sweeps through like a tidal wave! Now the room was alive with ideas. We had asked God for some of that Pentecostal power Jesus promised in Acts 1:8, and He wouldn't let us down. Sometimes pastors and other church leaders moan, "Well nothing happens in our church." Oh? Or, "Why won't the Holy Spirit move in our town?" Let me get this straight. You're asking why the Holy Spirit doesn't move? Are you kidding? Jesus told Nicodemus that the Holy Spirit was like the wind, *always* moving to and fro. But to feel that wind, you have to open a window! Let some fresh air in! Some churches haven't had fresh air come through since the Great Depression. And they're still depressed!

One of the staff members piped up to suggest, "Say, let's try to get low income people here and supply them with groceries. That would please the Lord!" Ah! What a terrific idea! That brought up the subject of the Convoy of Hope. A quick call to that corporate office assured us of their support with a truck they would dispatch bringing in twenty-five tons of nonperishable food to distribute on Easter morning. Other calls rounded up another thirty tons of perishable food from local sources. Altogether fifty-five tons of food would be available! (This is one of the reasons we needed the stadium all day Saturday, not only to set up all the staging, equipment, and auxiliary tents, but to package fifty-five tons of food! We ended up with several hundred church folks working all day Saturday, thrilled to be doing something so incredibly out of the ordinary for the sake of Jesus.)

The idea of distributing food to the needy brought up another problem. If people are struggling financially, how can they get to the stadium to receive the food? Sure, many of them had cars, but many did not. We certainly didn't have enough church vans or busses to go get them all. Now another staff member (see how contagious this is!)

came up with this idea: "Let's call the city bus transit company and request that they run every bus line on Easter Sunday right past the stadium. Fort Myers isn't that big, so maybe the city bus company would be amenable to such a request." Once again I picked up the phone and after a rather short conversation, in which I promised that we would give a great "plug" for the bus company that Easter morning, I learned that the utilities manager would be more than happy to assist in this humanitarian enterprise. Every bus route would pass by the stadium in time to get to the service and to pick people up afterward! That meant that anyone in the county who wanted to could come to our Easter service on a city bus for a couple of quarters.

Other issues arose: What size platform do we need? (Huge enough for 100 choir members, the band, special guests, and the pulpit.) What do we do for adequate sound in a stadium? Well . . . who does better stadium sound than rock n' roll groups? Getting them to help would give us inroads to that sector of our society. How do we advertise? How and where do we set up tents for children, ushers, seekers, etc.? Where do we get the chairs for those tents? Who sets them up? The list of assignments began. Remember: It's one thing to dream and quite another to implement. Yes, indeed, faith without works is dead.

> **It's one thing to dream and quite another to implement. Yes, indeed, faith without works is dead.**

A day or so later, I received a follow-up phone call from the fellow at the Twins' stadium. He asked, "Pastor, we have a ball game scheduled to start Easter Sunday afternoon at 3 o'clock. You must have the ball field cleared by then. Any problem?" I gulped a bit, but responded that it wouldn't be a problem at all. That meant tearing down a stage (which we built over second base), taking down a massive sound system (which I borrowed from the rock group), and removing any and all seats we had on the infield. "I have another question, Pastor. Two, actually: Do you have a young person who sings well who could sing the National Anthem prior to the start of the game and, second, do you have anyone else who could throw out the first pitch?" Well, we had any number of young people who could sing the song, and I knew of only one person who could/should throw out the first pitch. Ahem . . . need I elaborate? My arm is still sore. Wicked curve. The ball reached the catcher on only two bounces.

On the Saturday before Easter, workers came from everywhere to sack up fifty-five tons of food, set up tables outside the stadium for the lunch we would serve, and prepare the place for a church service. This included checking sound, setting up television cameras, printing song sheets (we didn't have projection available), equipping the tents for children's services and a nursery, setting up the long line of tables to dispense food and another line of tables and chairs to serve lunch following the service, and all the other vital services needed for such an event. But the workers were joyful, singing as they worked.

Easter morning dawned, and it was a gorgeous morning. Thank God! We had sincerely prayed for blue skies over the city. The temperature at service time would be seventy degrees under puffy white clouds. I stood on the stadium roof and watched cars drive into the parking lots—long, long lines of cars. Hundreds of cars! My heart jumped as folks began filing into the stadium. I could see the smoke from the barbecue pits in the lunch area. People began singing, long before the service started; on their own they began celebrating Christ's resurrection, lifting their voices in joyous song. What an opportunity God had given us! I had hired an aerial photographer to get good pictures from about a thousand feet up.

Well over 6,000 people attended the service. I had the privilege of preaching an Easter salvation message, and several hundred people responded to the invitation to accept Christ. Following the benediction, over 2,000 people lined up for the sacks of groceries we had prepared. They packed their cars with them. Others lugged them home on the city buses. Folks must have heard we were serving lunch because our workers counted 7,600 fed that day (a whole lot more than attended the service). While they were eating lunch, hundreds of our church folks cleared the diamond, even as the ballplayers began infield practice.

Our young singer gave a masterful touch on the National Anthem, and most people just laughed when I threw out the opening pitch.

What a fabulous day! Resurrection Day! Why shouldn't God's people celebrate such days of victory? The Holy Spirit has given Pentecostal believers the power to accomplish outlandish victories for Christ. We don't ask God to do it for us. He has given us the *power* to accomplish these tasks. Faith is necessary, of course, but so is a lot of hard work.

Not long ago, I preached a missions service on the east coast. It was in an alleged Pentecostal church. I say "alleged" because there was precious little evidence of the power Jesus promised in Acts 1:8. The service started twenty minutes late. (I learned that was pretty much the norm there.) There were about seventy-five people present, which meant 1,500 minutes were lost forever. Like "water spilled on the ground" (2 Sam. 14:14), that time could never be gathered up again. Then the worship team made its grand appearance giving a performance rather than leading the folks in singing. They chose to sing a song with these astounding lyrics:

> *Bring them in, Lord; bring them in.*
> *Bring them in, Lord; bring them in.*
> *Bring them in, Lord; bring them in.*

You already guessed the next line.

The song had neither musical nor theological merit. It was a total waste of everyone's time. When I finally got to the pulpit, I asked the folks, "Where in the world did you get that song? Nowhere in Scripture does God promise to 'bring them in.' Instead, He has given you and me the ability through the Holy Spirit to go into the highways and byways to bring people in ourselves. We're commissioned by our Lord for this task, and He isn't going to do it for us. Further, one day He will hold us accountable for how faithfully we obeyed that commission."

My, it got quiet in there . . . downright cold, as a matter of fact. For while they were playing church, singing meaningless music, and wasting the time of God's people, several hundred thousand people in their town were lost and headed for a Christ-less eternity. I thought to myself, *Why don't these professing Pentecostals get in the game and "play ball"?* There were multitudes of spiritual victories to be won.

It's professed by some that Nero played his fiddle while Rome burned. That may or may not be true, but I know something that is true: Many churches and believers just "fiddle" while people fall headlong into eternity. The truly sad thing is that we can make a difference, a huge one—but it takes vision, faith, and a whole lot of elbow grease.

CHAPTER  FOURTEEN

A DISTRICT CATCHES
THE VISION

I'VE NEVER BEEN A DISTRICT SUPERINTENDENT IN MY DENOMINATIONAL FELLOWSHIP (SOME DENOMINATIONS CALL THESE LEADERS BISHOPS, OVERSEERS, ETC.). I've never wanted to be one, so I've never allowed my name to stand for election for that office. Why? I suspect that being a district superintendent (in any church fellowship) may be the toughest job in the ministry. About the only reason anyone would ever contact you would be because they wanted something, had a complaint, or were in trouble of some sort. Besides, every four years you would be up for re-election. Hardly a case for job security! I've loved being a pastor! My cup is full.

However, I did spend sixteen years as an assistant district superintendent in the Peninsular Florida District of the Assemblies of God. It was kind of a fluke the way it happened. I surely wasn't expecting to hold the position. It was a foregone conclusion that another pastor was a shoo-in to be elected for the job, so my wife and I had already loaded up the car to head home from our district council. Someone came running out to the parking lot and hollered, "Hey, Betzer, you better get back in there. You're about to be elected assistant superintendent!" I couldn't believe it! But by the time we got back into the church, it was a *fait accompli*. Done, sealed, and delivered. I didn't want the job (even though it was a part-time task and wouldn't detract from my pastoring). But then it was explained to me that with the title came the portfolio of world missions director for the entire district (over 300 churches at the time). Ah! That made a huge difference to me, and I immediately accepted the responsibility. This portfolio would give me access to all of our churches with the aim of helping the district become a world-missions champion.

At that time our district was far down in the pack of Assemblies of God districts when it came to missions support. Yet we probably had more people attending our churches on Sunday morning than any other district in the nation. I truly believed that something remarkable could be done to motivate our pastors and churches to become mission leaders. I believed we could encourage congregations to set in motion actions that would impact millions of people around the world. I asked the Lord fervently for His direction in this eternal enterprise.

I'm grateful for the immediate support I received from the district superintendent and the presbytery. What I asked them for was quite outrageous. Our annual district council lasts for three days in May with services Monday through Wednesday. I had the temerity to request that the Tuesday night service be set aside solely for a world missions rally. I promised them that God had laid a plan on my heart that would raise millions of dollars in our churches for global evangelism. Praise the Lord, they bought the plan, lock, stock, and barrel. They caught the vision!

God's Plan for Our District

The plan God laid on my heart was simple.

1. *The presbytery would choose a missions project somewhere in the world.* I would go to that nation, along with a film crew, and we would make a video (a new concept at that time) of about four to six minutes. A video longer than that would fail our purpose. In the video, shot entirely on location, we would present the project or need. It might be an orphanage, a series of church buildings, a school, etc.

Well, there are videos . . . and then there are videos. Many missions DVD's I've seen are truly uninspired and nonproductive, so I picked the brains of some communication experts who knew what they were doing. The scripts we used were prayerfully and expertly designed and outstanding videographers knew how to make them come alive on video tape. They were truly professionally done. Why would we do anything less for the Master? Doesn't He deserve our very best?

We shot the video in Chennai, India, with my dear friend David Mohan, who preaches to about 50,000 in his church every weekend. Traditional church history has it that the apostle Thomas was martyred in that area. We opened the video with a dramatization of the murder, filmed on the spot where it was believed to have taken place. Many people told us that the martyrdom of Thomas launched what became a full-blown revival of Christianity in southeast India. (An interesting sidebar: When the stage blood was shed from the actor playing Thomas, it spilled over a rock and formed the exact shape of India.) It was the goal of Pastor Mohan (who also serves as the general superintendent of the Assemblies of God in India) to open 25,000 new churches within a decade. This, of course, necessitated many Bible training centers across the nation. Otherwise, where would the needed pastors originate? I titled the video, "The Thomas Factor."

2. *Upon returning home, I showed the finished video to our district presbytery, enlisting their support.* We produced five hundred copies of the video, and I mailed them personally to every pastor, evangelist, missionary, and other church leader in the district. The video had a professional jacket, printed in four-color. The packaging was extremely classy, which I believed would assist in getting pastors to open the mailing and play the video right away. I asked them to show the short video on a Sunday morning and then receive an offering for the project, which they would bring with them to the Tuesday night missions rally at district council. They could bring cash or faith promises.

3. *Now here is the key: We set a goal of at least a one million dollar offering on missions night at council.* To most pastors, churches, and key leaders this would have seemed impossible. Here is a key to raising that kind of money. The goal had to be broken down into bite-size pieces. I learned that we could open a church in India and train a new pastor for

a mere $8,000. It was my belief that virtually every church in our district could come up with $8,000, given sufficient time. I got the videos in the hands of the pastors in February and the council was in May. Surely every church, regardless of size, could produce $8,000 in that length of time. If they did, then well over two million dollars could be raised. It's not helpful to set a huge goal that a small church can't relate to. To tell a church leader of a tiny congregation, struggling to keep the lights on, that you want to raise a million dollars in one night would probably be difficult to receive. But even a church of fifty people or less could raise $8,000 in several months. I encouraged pastors of even small churches to challenge their people: "You know, we can make a difference in India for all eternity. Though we are just a few people, we can raise $8,000 between now and district council! Let's plant a church in that nation!" It was amazing how many people responded to that! It was something they could do for Jesus they hadn't even thought of before.

4. *A vital part of this plan was the rally on Tuesday night.* I wanted a great number of people there, both clergy and laity! That meant the service had to be incredible and deeply moving. I wanted the district missions night to become a highlight of every council. To that end I enlisted a lot of people to plan and participate. The rally for India, for example, was held in a hotel in Orlando. How could we make the night simply spiritually stunning, unforgettable, and life-changing?

In our church, as is the case with many churches in our fellowship, we have a Master's Commission (which is now called the Florida School of Discipleship). We had about seventy-five students at the time: gifted, hard-working kids who would do anything for God. And they were extraordinarily talented! We had a few planning meetings to plumb for ideas, practical ways of implementing them, and to pray for fulfillment of our visionary goals. The students arrived in Orlando early the day of the Tuesday night rally. They brought trunkloads of clothes they had created to look like the common apparel of people in India. They spent hours putting on makeup, transforming themselves from American kids to southern Asians. I didn't recognize most of them when they were done.

As people arrived at the service that night, they were met by scores of beggars, lepers, and dying "Indians" begging for help. When people entered the hotel restrooms they saw poor, dying people lying on the floors or under the sinks. Some of them were wrapped in old newspapers. The delegates were accosted in the hallways by people who didn't always smell the best and certainly weren't folks you would choose to sit by in the service. (Yes, they were our Master's Commission kids!) In other words, everyone who came to the district missions rally was transported by our kids to southern India. Many of the delegates entered the meeting hall in a state of shock. (Some were upset because they didn't realize their "accosters" were kids in costume. They thought district council had been overcome by "foreigners.")

I had earlier called Pastor Mohan for a list of great Indian musicians and we flew over a team of worship leaders from Chennai who dressed in Indian garments and played Indian instruments, as they led the thousand or so people in the service in songs such as would be sung in Delhi or Chennai. We purposely did not include any typical American music. Everything had to convey the feeling of India. Some talented local actors presented a short drama that depicted the plight of nearly a billion people in India, lost and headed for hell. We also flew in David Mohan to preach. You may be thinking, *Well, that was a lot of work!* You aren't kidding, and I haven't even told you the whole story here.

Was it worth it? The offering that night in cash and faith promises neared $2 million to open churches in India. The evening set our district buzzing! Many pastors went home with a new burden for the lost overseas. They also went home with the knowledge that *presenting missions is not boring!* Many began planning how they could transform their congregations from mediocrity (or worse) in a missions burden to faithful commitment to Christ's Great Commission. Within just a few years, our district giving vaulted from middle-of-the-pack nationally to the top spot in all the Assemblies of God, where it remains today. Seven of our Florida churches rank in the top 100 missions-giving churches in the nation.

There Are No Valid Excuses

I hear this nagging refrain so often in my travels, "Well, there just isn't enough money." The truth is there is so much money in this country it's staggering. It just

It's the role of a pastor to set the stage, to cast the vision.

has to be mined, sought for, and produced. Or I hear, "Well, we just don't have the people to do some of these things." I respond, "How do you know that? Have you tried?" It's the role of a pastor to set the stage, to cast the vision. Most congregations are a reflection of their pastor.

Other times I hear, "Well, Dan, that might work for you because your church is large." Listen! All the principles I use I learned as a home-missions pastor in Ohio. My first pastoral pulpit was a Maytag washer in the basement of our home on the southern shore of Lake Erie. The congregation was a handful of people sitting in old, creaking folding chairs. But I knew something basic and it was this: There are many men and women of financial means, leadership charisma, and influence in my community. These people, for the most part, aren't going to attend a church without a vision, where they see evidence of little or no hard work. You see, these successful people didn't attain their stratosphere in life by lack of faith, little hard work, and thinking there was no possibility of success. They won't attend or become members of a congregation without a strong work ethic and vision.

"But . . . but . . . we don't have any money in our little church!" Oh, how often I've heard that! I make this statement (and I can back it up!): Every miracle of provision I've seen in decades of pastoring I can attribute to *missions*! Jesus said that signs and wonders would follow those who believe and act upon it. The signs and wonders never precede; they follow! You can readily understand then why *faith* is so vital. Without such faith it is impossible to please God (Heb. 11:6). I can list many reasons why our church can't possibly make it in the natural for we have very few wealthy people. But Pentecostal churches don't wallow in the natural. Pentecost introduces Christ's followers to the supernatural.

When God led the children of Israel out of Egyptian slavery, they took with them the fortunes of many Egyptians who gladly gave them such possessions. Those citizens of the Nile wanted relief from the plagues. I fully understand that churches battle financial challenges much of the time, but we are surrounded by vast wealth in the "Egypt" around us that needs to be "mined" for Christ.

I'll give you an example. Our entire fellowship normally gives about $200 million annually to missions. Some think that's a pretty big deal. It depends how you look at it. We have nearly 12,500 churches in this country, quite a few of them that give a million dollars or more annually. Many give nothing. So when you divide $200 million by the number of potential church givers, that figure isn't really all that impressive.

How so? My son, who spent seventeen years as a missionary in South Africa, was in a meeting in Fort Lauderdale recently. One day he went to the harbor to watch the ships come in. Along came a magnificent private yacht. My son found it was the property of a couple who were the only two passengers on this ocean-going craft. It carried a crew of about twenty. When it was moored, David found the owner to learn more about the ship. He learned that it cost over $80,000 just to fill the fuel tanks. He had the nerve to ask the owner how much he paid for the ship. The answer? $225,000,000! For one "boat" for one couple!

When David related that story to me I moaned inwardly. One couple paid more for one boat than 12,500 Pentecostal churches gave collectively for missions in one whole year. "But, but, Dan, our churches don't have money like that!" I understand that, but "Egypt" all around us *does*! There's so much wealth around us that it's shocking. Church leader, don't moan and groan about how tough times are! Lift up your eyes and look on the harvest field and pray to God for ways of provision for the harvest. Are we infiltrating our Egypt? Are we making contacts that could change the face of missions around the world? I believe the supply is there. As my friend Tommy Barnett preaches, "The miracle is in the house!"

CHAPTER **FIFTEEN**

THE WALGREENS PRINCIPLE

SOMEONE POINTED OUT TO ME NOT LONG AGO THAT THE
BRAINS OF MEN ARE COMPOSED OF LITTLE BOXES, FROM
WHICH THERE IS LITTLE OR NO ESCAPE. (I think it was a lady
who told me that.) I laughed at the premise, but it could well be true—
especially of us pastors. Our compartmentalized craniums get divided
like over-crowded housing developments with ecclesiastical details,
so much so that when God wants to transplant a really large idea into
our brains we think we can't handle it. There are too many little boxes
to be negotiated. This is where we must utilize the faith principle of
Hebrews 11. Leaders must allow God to show them "things not yet
seen." And then act on them!

One day I was driving down a main thoroughfare of our
community when I saw a corner lot that had been leveled and had
a big sign that declared, "Coming Soon—Another Walgreens Drug
Store Near You!" I remember making some disparaging noise and
thinking, *Great, that's just what we need ... another Walgreens Drug Store!
We have so many of them in Florida now that soon every family will have its
own private pharmacy.*

At that moment the Lord rebuked me, asking, "Dan, how come
you're not as smart as the people at Walgreens?" Well, I took a bit of
umbrage at that put-down. "What do you mean, Lord? How am I not
that smart?" Here was the response. "Take a look at what you're doing,
Dan. You're on television every day asking people to come to First

Assembly of God in Fort Myers. Most of the people you are talking to live within a hundred-mile radius of the church. Now, just how did you expect them to get there?" And the rebuke continued: "Dan, take note carefully: There isn't just *one* Walgreens in your town. There isn't just *one* Walmart. There isn't just *one* McDonalds. These stores are everywhere. Why? So people can get to them. Now, how come you're not that smart? Why don't you plant churches all over the area so people can get to them?"

Plant a church? Well, I could give the Lord a whole lot of reasons why we weren't going to plant a church. Such a venture would cost money! Lots of money! It would take people out of our congregation ("And, Lord, you know how hard we worked to get them there in the first place!") It would require searching for good leadership, which is a major job in itself! I went on and on, telling the Lord why planting churches just was not in our plans.

Still the Lord kept asking me, "Dan, how come you're not as smart as the people at Walgreens?" On our daily TV programs I continued to invite people to come to our sanctuary and in my mind I would hear that nagging word, "Walgreens." In other words, "Go where the people are!" I should have instinctively known that. Jesus' story of the Good Samaritan (Luke 10) made that so clear. He told about the wayfaring man headed for Jericho who was beaten up, robbed, stripped of his garments, and left beside the road to die. Several religious people passed him by, not wanting to get involved. Then a Samaritan came his way. Gasping for every possible breath, the dying fellow couldn't come to the Samaritan, so the Samaritan came to him! How simple can that principle be?

But a certain Samaritan, as he journeyed, came where he was. And when he saw him, he had compassion. *So he went to him* and bandaged his wounds, pouring on oil and wine; and he set him on his own animal, brought him to an inn, and took care of him.(Luke 10:33–34, emphasis mine)

My late friend, Missionary Morris Williams, told me he thought of the Samaritan as Jesus, the dying man as the world, and the inn as the church. Jesus picks up dying humanity, brings them to the church and commands, "Here, take care of them! Spend what you have to! I'll pay you back when I return!" Isn't that what Jesus has promised us as well? This lifetime is not our payday. The effective Christian leader will rarely be reimbursed commensurately in this life time; that comes in eternity. You're not "home" yet. Payday is coming over there, not here. As a pastor I complained, "Lord, planting a church costs money—and people!" And in my spirit I could hear the Lord say, "Spend whatever you have to! When I come again, I will repay you!" That lit my fire!

> **Do I really expect these victims who are spiritually dying by the side of the road to come to us, all slicked up, shoes shined, and beaming from ear to ear? Hardly!**

My late mentor, Oswald Smith, used to drum into me, "Dan, God will never owe you anything—not money, not time, not people! Do what is needed to get the evangelism job done!" All over our part of Florida there are people whom Satan has beaten to the proverbial bloody pulp. We find them everywhere, bound by booze, drugs, pornography, bad home situations, lost incomes, poverty, disease, despair, you name it. Do I really expect these victims who are spiritually dying by the side of the road to come to us, all slicked up, shoes shined, and beaming from ear to ear? Hardly! We need to go to them, to where they are, and in Jesus' name bind up their wounds and attend to their needs. Is it messy? Sometimes. Is it costly? Usually. Is it worth it? The angels of heaven shout yes for every lost soul who comes home!

Planting New Churches

I thank the Lord for a church board (church council) willing to show forth hearts of compassion and faith. I told the Lord, and then the board, that we were going to be "Walgreens people." They unanimously supported this concept of faith. So we got to work, planting the first church just across the river that divides Fort Myers from burgeoning Cape Coral. That was just the start. In the intervening years we have planted a number of churches in our part of Florida: Kingsway Assembly of God in Cape Coral; First Assembly Spanish in Miami (in the heart of Little Havana); Life Church in Sarasota; First Assembly Cornerstone in Fort Myers; First Assembly Spanish in Fort Myers; River of Life in Estero; First Assembly West in Cape Coral; and First Assembly Care Ministries.

In that latter ministry, we have a full-time pastor who has organized a strong core of scores of dedicated workers who hold regular services in over fifty nursing homes every week—same time, same personnel. (Did we really expect those infirm senior citizens to come to our church? Impossible!) We minister to over 1,200 of those older folks confined to those homes every week. Some become members of First Assembly. Some receive water baptism. They take communion. They are a somewhat "rotating congregation" because so many slip into eternity from week to week. During the past several years, hundreds of those residents of care facilities have accepted Christ, and over half of those people have since died and gone into eternity. What if we weren't there? What if we had just declared: "Well, they can't get to church, so . . . that's that"? Should we have ignored them simply because they couldn't jump in their cars to get to our church? Is this ministry costly? Oh, yes. Is it time-consuming? More than you could believe. Is it worth it? Most assuredly!

We have called these church plants "satellite campuses." I learned the hard way that you can't just start a church, put a neophyte in the pulpit as pastor, and hope for the best. The planting church must watch over the new foundling as surely as a mother cares for her infant. A planting pastor must find leadership in the new church willing to agree to the DNA that made the founding church so successful, which sounds a whole lot easier than it actually is.

Sometimes young pastors come out of Bible college thinking they have every known answer to every known problem but soon show—they don't have! That's why we've gone with the principle of satellites. The pastors we bring in to lead the new churches have to understand that for at least a year or two, our First Assembly church council is their board as well. Our stated philosophy must be their philosophy. For example: I have already declared in this book that the pursuit of missions is our priority. Frankly, it grows more difficult to find new or young leadership who understand that. I've had some prospects tell me, "Well, Pastor Betzer, I believe our mission is our community." They don't get hired here because they're only partly correct. Jesus said the whole world, Jerusalem, Judea, Samaria, and the uttermost parts of the world are our mission field. I would never bring a leader to one of our satellites who was not totally committed to global evangelization—and who exhibited the faith to make that commitment work.

In the satellites we have "seeded" the new congregations both with funding and with people. We have sent as many as 125 persons to launch the new works. How do we do that? I require the one selected as pastor for the planted church to serve on my staff for at least six months, attending our pastoral staff meetings, attending board meetings, working side by side with me, preaching whenever proper, and learning what we do and how we do it. On a highly profiled Sunday, that young pastor preaches to the main church congregation, closing with this invitation: "Next week we start 'such and such' church. We need people to go with us. We need people to give this morning in a seed offering to launch the work. I will ask everyone who feels led by the Lord to go with us to stand up now and, following the offering, walk out the door with me!"

I recall the first time we followed that trail. The new planting pastor we hired was good, so I figured that perhaps twenty people would want to join the church plant. Imagine my shock when he gave the invitation to join him in the new work and over 100 people stood up and walked out the door (one of them a board member and twelve of them members of the sanctuary choir). I remembered an old western movie in which someone called out, "Come back, Shane!" I wanted to call out, "Come back! Let's talk this over!" You know, we pastors are pretty good at math, and I was watching tithe payers leave us . . . at least $7,000 a week in tithes and offerings! "Come back, Shane!" Then I remembered what Dr. Oswald J. Smith had pounded into me, "God will never owe you anything!" You know what happened? The next week the choir was full again. I didn't see any vacant seats in our sanctuary where the 100 had been the week before, and the general fund offering was a record-breaker. Jesus was prophetic when He said signs and wonders would follow those who were obedient to His call to reach the world.

Many hundreds of churches could easily plant a new work in their areas this year. It sounds scary and, frankly, it is a bit. But with every new church plant, our church has been blessed and increased. God will be debtor to no person!

Today half of those churches are now fully independent congregations within our Assemblies of God fellowship. Placed altogether, those aforementioned congregations now minister to well over 3,200 persons every Lord's day. We "seeded" those congregations with perhaps 300–400 persons, total. What an investment! About ten persons have come into God's kingdom for every person who left our congregation, and our own church has grown as well.

You know, those folks at Walgreens are smarter than we think. They go where the people are. The church of Jesus Christ ought to be at least that smart, don't you think? Could your congregation plant a church this year? Probably. Would God bless such an effort? Unquestionably. Pray about it, and if you hear the word *Walgreens* in your mind and heart, it didn't come from me.

CHAPTER 🌿 SIXTEEN

A BANQUET OR A PICNIC?

On SEVERAL OCCASIONS I'VE TRIED TO BE LIKE MOSES AND CLIMB MOUNT SINAI—OR AT LEAST THE PLACE GENERALLY ACKNOWLEDGED TO BE THE HOLY MOUNTAIN, SAINT CATHERINE IN THE SOUTHERN SINAI PENINSULA. I haven't succeeded . . . not even with the help of a willing, but odorous, camel that painfully bore my body two-thirds of the way. (The saddle, by the way, was meant for a six-year-old child. By the time I dismounted I needed a chiropractor just to walk.)

Through the years, a steep pathway has been secured toward the summit, starting at the Saint Catherine Monastery and ending at the summit. It's a treacherous trek over loose rock, past turns along dangerous precipices. But Moses climbed to the top without the prepared pathway or the miserable camel, and he was eighty! The book of Exodus tells the dramatic tale:

> Then the Lord said to Moses, "Come up to Me on the mountain and be there; and I will give you tablets of stone, and the law and commandments which I have written, that you may teach them." Then Moses went up to the mountain, and a cloud covered the mountain. Now the glory of the Lord rested on mount Sinai, and the cloud covered it six days. And on the seventh day He called to Moses out of the midst of the cloud. The sight of the glory of the Lord was like

a consuming fire on the top of the mountain in the eyes of the children of Israel. So Moses went into the midst of the cloud and went up into the mountain. And Moses was on the mountain forty days and forty nights. (Exod. 24:12, 15–18)

Not only was the climb dangerous, but the summit appeared to be on fire. Still the great man climbed. Moses was with the Lord atop that mountain for around six weeks. There he received the Ten Commandments. He gained not only those awesome tablets of stone, but God also gave him the plans and specifications to build the tabernacle. This would be the portable worship center for the children of Israel until that time nearly five centuries later when King Solomon would construct the first temple in Jerusalem. God had specific instructions about the construction materials for the tabernacle. An "anything goes . . . it's just for the church" attitude was definitely not allowed. Among the requirements:

And this is the offering which you shall take from them: gold, silver, and bronze; blue, purple, and scarlet thread, fine linen, and goats' hair; rams skins dyed red, badgers skins, and acacia wood; oil for the light, and spices for the anointing oil and for the sweet incense; onyx stones, and stones to be set in the ephod and in the breastplate. And let them make Me a sanctuary that I may dwell among them. (Exod. 25:3–8)

Note carefully that God required *fine linen!* Not old rags, not cheap cloth, not hand-me-downs. Fine linen! The best they had!

I once saw a very funny cartoon in a church magazine. It showed a native tribe somewhere in Africa opening a missionary barrel that had been shipped to them by ladies in an American church. These precious saints had taken old sheets, laundered them, and then had torn them into strips and rolled them up for potential bandages. So the puzzled natives looked at them, totally not knowing what they were for. The chief picked one up and said, "I don't know what these are, but maybe we could sew them together and make sheets out of them."

Somewhere many Christian believers have got the idea that, "Hey, it's just for the church, so . . . whatever! Let's just tear up some old sheets. Let's just make a half-effort. It's just for the Lord, isn't it?" What about "fine linen"? Where did we get the idea that God would be thrilled with our second-hand efforts and junk?

Earlier in this book, I related how the home-missions church I pastored in Ohio bought the downtown bank building, a phenomenal four-story structure made of imported marble. The news media made a big deal out of it and, as a result, I received a lot of phone calls and inquiries. One such call came to my study from a lady who wanted to make a contribution. She said, "Pastor Betzer, I don't attend your church, but I've been reading in the local newspaper about your acquisition of the bank and I'd like to give the church something. We have an old, beat-up, piano in our home. It needs a lot of work and isn't very playable. We've just bought a fabulous new piano, and we'd like to donate the old piano to your church."

Now we pastors have been trained in public relations. I knew I was supposed to respond to this lady: "Oh, thank you! Bless you! We're so grateful!" We call it tact; God calls it lying! So I responded, "Ma'am, thanks for calling, but we really don't want that beat-up piano in this church. We would be glad, however, to receive your new piano." Wham! She hung up.

Several days later, one of the staff burst into my office to announce, "Pastor, there's a moving van downstairs, and they're bringing a new piano inside." I thought to myself, *Well, the piano people are confused. They've confused the order.* So I called the lady back. I said to her, "Ma'am, there apparently is a mix-up with your piano. There are movers downstairs bringing your new piano into the church. I just wanted you to . . ."

She interrupted, "No, no . . . there's no mistake." And I could tell she was sniffling. "No mistake, Pastor. I didn't sleep all night after talking to you. I got to thinking that we were giving God's church junk and were keeping the good piano for ourselves. So the new piano is for the church!" Yes! Of course! That's the principle that should always be in effect when it comes to service for the Lord. We give God "fine linen."

In the years I was the speaker on the network broadcast *Revivaltime*, I was privileged to speak in hundreds of churches. I often saw the following scenario: The pastor would announce, "Before our speaker comes, brother (or sister) so-and-so will sing." The singer would invariably grab the microphone and blow into it, or tap it, and ask, "Is this on?" It often was not. Or the volume level was either so low you couldn't hear the singer or so loud it would howl and screech. Then the singer would say, "Now you all pray for me as I try to sing (what does that mean: "try to sing") because I haven't had time to practice." And I would say to myself about the singer, "If you haven't practiced, get off the platform! What do you think this is, God's karaoke hour?" I can't imagine a pop singer saying something so insipid. Can you conceive a Vegas nightclub singer informing the crowd, "I haven't practiced"? Not a chance. Well, you protest, "No, but look what that singer in Vegas is being paid!" Listen, child of God, what do you think *you're* being paid? By all eternal standards you make that Vegas entertainer look like a pauper! So give God your "fine linen"! He isn't interested in your castoffs, your lethargic efforts. He wants your "fine linen."

This principle holds true for us pastors as well. I've heard sermons that were read (badly), obviously prepared by someone else. When a pastor stands before a congregation, that pastor should have spent hours with God in the study, preparing a spiritual meal (meat!) for the parishioners that will sustain them in their journey. It requires hours of hard work to do that. It's "fine linen"!

A Banquet Fit for the King

You may be wondering, "Well, what does this have to do with missions?" Everything! Recently I spoke at a church missions banquet in the eastern United States. The pastor had contacted me about a year ago, asking if I would fly out there for the event. When I told him my stipulations (not my own financial requirements, for that is never a factor, but the way in which I wanted the banquet to function), he gulped a bit and said, "Okay." The result was about a million dollars in cash and faith promises for global evangelism. His first ideas about the night were certainly not "fine linen." Nor was it going to be a banquet. It was going to be, at best, a picnic. You know—butcher paper on the tables, paper plates, cardboard drinking cups, and plastic "silverware."

Listen, I don't care how spiritual a congregation or audience is, after they've tried to eat a steak with a plastic knife and fork, they've long since lost the victory by the time the speaker begins his plea. Nor do I ever speak at a missions banquet where the folks have brought in a "covered dish taste of the nations." (There's a reason why the dishes are covered!) I have seen some of the most awful cuisine imaginable in these ordeals. Such events are *not* banquets; they're not even good picnics. (And often should be followed by a divine healing service.) Yet they're done in the "name" of the King. If you announce a banquet, be honest and have a banquet! A little "truth in advertising" in God's house would be most helpful.

There are other stipulations to a successful banquet. I gained this valuable information years ago while serving as associate evangelist for that marvelous Methodist revivalist, Dr. Ford Philpot. At that time, his ministry was probably second only to the Billy Graham evangelistic crusades. Ford's headquarters were in Lexington, Kentucky. We (our team of seven) traveled over various parts of the world holding citywide or countywide crusades. Dr. Philpot had the first syndicated color Christian television series in this country called *The Story*. I wrote and produced it. I also edited his magazine *The Storyteller*; I was master of ceremonies for the TV program; sang with his crusade trio, The Fishermen; preached when Ford couldn't for one reason or another; and set up his crusades. It required the better part of a year to prepare for such endeavors. By the time a stadium or arena was rented, advertising secured, literature printed, preparatory meetings held weeks in advance, travel plans and housing obtained, and a long list of other necessary expenditures taken care of, thousands upon thousands of dollars were spent. But we never had to push for funds in the actual crusade because we never opened a crusade that wasn't already paid for, the money in the bank. That allowed us to receive offerings during the crusades for local needs of the churches. So where did those thousands of dollars come from? The banquets! I can report to you from experience that a blunder in the banquet could almost ruin the evangelistic endeavor.

Here are some of the things I learned (and the principles detailed here will fit many other endeavors for the Lord in your church):

• *Set a financial goal at the banquet.* I won't speak at any missions banquet unless the pastor has set a goal . . . and one that requires *faith!* What's the point of all the effort if there isn't a reason for it? "Well, don't folks get nervous with such goals?" Sometimes they do, but that's because they haven't been taught about faith or Christ's emphasis on His Great Commission. You know, we followers of His aren't given latitude in obeying His instructions. The goal needs to be announced, and the reason for it made clear. People don't usually respond to what Scripture calls "an uncertain sound" (1 Cor. 14:8 KJV).

• *The quality of the banquet must be representative of our King.* Use beautiful table cloths, silverware, glass goblets, china plates, floral center pieces, professionally and cleverly-printed programs, etc. "Well, that costs money!" Yes, it does (though some of these things can be borrowed from church folks). But it produces money! After all, remember this is a banquet on behalf of the King, not a picnic outing for some nondescript person. The very fact that a church leadership cares enough to make the banquet memorable and offer the very best attracts people from the community, if done on a regular and faithful basis. People get excited about these evenings; yes, even those doing the preparation for it, because they have seldom been a part of such a noble and out-of-the-ordinary venture. As people enter the banquet hall (and it can be in a church basement, if done properly), you can hear them saying, "Ooohh" and "Aaahh." They realize from the start they're going to experience something special.

• *Begin the banquet on time.* If the banquet is announced to start at 6:30 p.m., it *must* start at 6:30—on the dot. Don't waste people's time. If you have 100 people attend, and you start the banquet at 6:40, it may be only ten minutes late but you have wasted a thousand minutes that can never be salvaged (100 x 10 = 1,000). This principle holds true for all church meetings, by the way.

• *Music should be about missions* That's why we're there. "But . . . but we're supposed to worship!" How? By singing endless and aimless choruses that have precious little to do with missions? Or by obedience to our Lord's command to reach the world? In a recent banquet where I was privileged to speak at the church home of the famed gospel singers The Couriers, Neil Enloe and the group sang a song he wrote that truly reflected why we were there:

Only aliens and strangers and foreigners in danger,
They daily run the risk of losing all.
They're our substitutes at large for our Great Commission charge;
So we prayerfully support them in their call.

Chorus:
Missionaries, missionaries, taking families abroad
With a call to follow God.
Missionaries, visionaries—living martyrs who have died
*   to earthly dreams.*

With compassion for the lost, to win at any cost,
See the millions who are dying without Christ.
Be they hungry, sick or wounded, their search for help is ended
When the missionary comes to bring them life.

135

On that final judgment day, with all pretense swept away
And our works are tried by fire the final test;
Heaven's heroes on parade for their sacrifices made;
Missionaries will be leading all the rest.

When the trio finished that song, every one of the hundreds of people gathered knew exactly why we were there. The Couriers' song had set the stage for the Word to follow.

This whole chapter is dedicated to the principle of giving God our "fine linen" and not old rags. Our sanctuary in Fort Myers is now almost forty years old. The architecture is very dated; however, it's sparkling clean. The windows shine. The grass is mowed. The shrubs are trimmed. All the lights work. The carpets are vacuumed. The walls are painted. We offer God the "fine linen" of our efforts to cause His house to be reflective of our love for Him.

The church is blessed that honors God and gives Him "fine linen" in every endeavor.

There's a memorable story about King David in 2 Samuel 24. The king wanted to purchase a threshing floor (which would become a part of Jerusalem) from a farmer named Araunah. The farmer didn't want to take money for the purchase and offered it to David for nothing. The king's response is notable:

> "All these, O king, Araunah has given to the king." And Araunah said to the king, "May the LORD your God accept you." Then the king said to Araunah, "No, but I will surely buy it from you for a price; nor will I offer burnt offerings to the LORD my God with that which costs me nothing." So David bought the threshing floor and the oxen for fifty shekels of silver. (2 Samuel 24:23–24)

Let's be honest. Don't we all on occasion offer God something that costs us nothing? Instead of presenting the banquet sacrifice of our efforts, we offer picnics . . . ants and all. Yet we are the same people who loudly sing on Sunday morning, "He is worthy!" Worthy of what? A banquet, not a picnic.

The church is blessed that honors God and gives Him "fine linen" in every endeavor. Only our very best is good enough to lay at Jesus' feet.

CHAPTER  SEVENTEEN

THE BLESSED CHURCH HAS
A BIBLICAL WORLDVIEW

WHAT IS A BIBLICAL WORLDVIEW? It means perceiving the world and all the people in it the same way God perceives them. Note carefully the words, "In the same way God perceives them." That perception is often at odds with human concepts. The church leadership will have to decide whose perceptions to follow, those of people or of God.

Sadly, according to recent polls very few gospel-preaching churches have such a view. The Barna Research Group reports that many of our moral and spiritual challenges are directly attributable to the absence of a biblical world view. The 2003 survey of over two thousand professing followers of Christ showed that only a relative handful had such a perspective. A mere 4 percent of unchurched Americans had any comprehension of it, and, astoundingly, only 9 percent of professing believers in Christ knew much about it. That figure can be broken down as follows: 7 percent of Protestants in general, 2 percent of those adults attending mainline churches, and fewer than 2 percent of Roman Catholics have a biblical worldview. The only "redeeming" factor is those Spirit-filled and anointed churches who believe passionately about missions, which brings the 9 percent figure overall into reality [7]

Every gospel-believing pastor, leader, and church-attender

needs to reexamine his or her life and ministry philosophy carefully, prayerfully, and scripturally. Are we deceived? The Pharisees and Sadducees of Jesus' day sincerely believed they had the correct perception about God, but Jesus said they were deceived because they didn't know the Scriptures.

Jesus told His followers to blanket the world—yes, the uttermost parts of the world—with His gospel.

In my ministerial travels in the United States, I'm saddened and truly stunned sometimes at the provincial view of church leaders. The commission Christ gave us has been watered down from a worldview to a local view. Following His glorious resurrection from the dead, Jesus told His followers to blanket the world—yes, the uttermost parts of the world—with His gospel. Without the aid of the internet, social media, the printed page, and so many other benefits we enjoy today, those Spirit-filled followers of Jesus journeyed from Spain to Iraq, often (usually) at the expense of their own lives. Only the beloved John of the original twelve apostles died a natural death. The others gave their lives in obedience to the Great Commission.

The cost of the lack of a worldview in a local church is staggering. For one thing, it clogs the supernatural flow of God's provision to the congregation. Also, it restricts the outlook of the believers in that church from 360 degrees to a fraction of God's view. They see only the local situation, the church building, the musicians who may or may not be on key and properly motivated, the perceived ineptitude of the leadership, the length of the service, or the comfort of the pew. Their eyes are blindfolded, so they can't see the world as God sees it. As a result, the work for the Lord often becomes perfunctory. The "drive" is gone. The passion is missing! The concept of reaching multitudes of lost and hurting people is fleeting, if it exists at all.

One of my spiritual "dads," the late Leonard Ravenhill, used to drum into me, "Dan, preach the eternities!" I would stay for days in his home in Texas, and we would study and pray together with a passion that almost took my breath away. Others would come by such as evangelist Steve Hill and David Wilkerson, both now with the Lord, and Ravenhill's vision for the whole world infected our very souls! We didn't dare limit the pulpit or the church leadership to things that (as Ravenhill put it succinctly) "didn't amount to a hill of beans."

The effect of a godly worldview impacts a congregation in so many ways:

Issues that can negatively affect a congregation never or rarely see the light of day. People don't care what color the church carpet is, how people are dressed, or whether the choir is robed . . . or even if there is a choir. These are peripheral issues that possibly touch on personal opinion but never impact the effect of the church as a whole. Another Ravenhill-ism was, "Are the things you're living for worth Christ's dying for?" Jesus had such a passion for the lost of the world that He was willing to be crucified for them. What are we willing to do?

The people rejoice in giving. We often take two offerings in a service—one for the general fund and our missions program at-large, and the other for special needs. People who love to give don't object to multiple opportunities to do so. Rather they see the second offering as another way to be a blessing to folks at home and around the world. In my first weeks as pastor here in Fort Meyers, I took a second offering one Sunday and a board member upbraided me in our next council meeting. He said firmly, "We only take one offering here in each service and you will not take two." I watched several of the other members nod in agreement. I smiled at them, picked up my notes and pencil and put them in my briefcase and stood to leave. I said, "Now, you folks elected me a few weeks ago to be your pastor. I had clearly informed you when I came here as a candidate what my intentions would be, how I would go about implementing them, and my commitment to a godly worldview. I'm going home now and going to bed. You decide in the next few minutes if I'm your pastor, your leader or not, and you can let me know tomorrow. I have many things to do in this life and debating over a second offering is not one of them. Good night." And I left. As you might expect, that issue never came up again. In the meantime, millions of dollars have been given for needs at home and around the world through this local congregation. (Oh, the church at that time was running about 600 in attendance each weekend; as of this writing, the average is 6,269. People are drawn to a congregation that has passion and reaches out to the world.)

A giving church attracts people who are successful. In every city, town, or hamlet, there are people who "hear different music." They aren't "in tune" with mediocrity. They're successful because of their outlook on life. Some of these have great financial resources. Others command outstanding respect and leadership locally. Their influence is profound. They "feed" off realizing their place in society, their abilities, and opportunities. They won't be part of a church that can't see past the end of its proverbial nose. They have no interest in "churchy" issues that aren't important, but they're intrinsically drawn to on-fire congregations that see as God sees, to congregations that realize their place in this world and do something about situations, great or small, in a way that pleases the Lord. How do I know this? Because I see it all the time! Because we are blessed to be on local TV here every day, and have been for nearly twenty years, people come to me in malls, restaurants, on the street, etc., just to talk. They open their hearts to me. They send me letters and emails expressing their appreciation for this church that always extends an open hand to the needy and has a passion for the whole world. No, they don't all come swarming to First Assembly, but they express appreciation for the church and its members and adherents. Amazingly, they have an impact on their own churches. One local church here, a Spirit-filled Methodist church, has jumped from several hundred in attendance to well over 3,000 while pursuing our First Assembly philosophy of ministry, blessed by the Holy Spirit. Their pastor is now a leading missionary statesman in that denomination. Yes, a godly worldview is contagious!

There is purpose and stability in the church body with a godly worldview. I can't remember the last time I heard an unkind word spoken or saw one written within our congregation. Do we always agree on every issue? No, of course not! But we discuss differences of opinion civilly, gently, and in Christian love. Why is this? Because we're too strongly united on the main issue of embracing a godly worldview to get bogged down in peripheral issues that aren't eternally important.

One of the most meaningful parts of my ministerial life is the association our congregation celebrates with the Jewish community. I've spoken in most of the synagogues in our area in their Friday night Shabbat services, and some of the rabbis frequently visit my study just to talk and be encouraged. I've had the privilege of spending well over a year of my life in Israel, so I know the country fairly well. It's been a worthwhile pursuit to gain a working knowledge of Judaism, which, after all, is our root structure in Christianity and which Christ came to fulfill—not destroy. (However, I draw the line at eating Gefilte fish! I mean . . . there are limits!) My name Daniel Betzer is very Jewish and, in fact, many relatives of the late and great Israeli General Moshe Dayan were Betzers. Interestingly, a small river that flows through a canyon in Northwest Israel near the border with Lebanon is known as the Betzer

River. Darlene and I have walked softly through the former Nazi death camps in Germany and Poland and wept through our annual walks through the Yad Vashem Holocaust Museum in Jerusalem. For many reasons I have purposefully reached out to the Jewish community. So much so that when the Jewish Federation of Southwest Florida printed its phone and address book of area Jews, they included Darlene and me!

None of this would have happened if our church hadn't reached out to the Jewish community. Jesus was a Jew. The early Christian believers were Jews. So don't you find it a bit strange that many evangelical churches in America have little or no contact with the Jews and synagogues in their communities? They isolate themselves. Is it because of fear? Or lack of concern? Or lack of knowledge? I only know such congregations are deprived of some of the most precious experiences of life: touching people for whom Jesus died.

The local Muslim Imam is also a friend of mine. We have had dinner in his home. I invited him to speak on Islam in our church (before a packed crowd), flanked by a former Muslim who debated him on the main issues of that religion. The Imam and I hardly agree on anything. Our first contact point came when I learned that he was a native of Damascus, Syria. I've spent some time in that ancient, biblical city, even walking down the street called Straight (spoken of in Acts 9:11). You see, when we have a worldview, we look for connecting points with those outside our faith. And how I love to talk to atheists! It's been my privilege to lead some of them to saving grace in Christ. How can I just "write these people off" because of the canyons of differences in our belief systems?

Over and over we are told in Scripture that God is not willing that anybody perish. Now think about that! If He isn't willing for the lost to die in their unbelief, there must be some way to reach them. Otherwise, He would be cruel and arbitrary. As a pastor I have to believe that everyone in our community is a prime candidate for God's salvation. That belief fuels virtually everything we do. For example our town is a tourist town. There are quite a few adult night clubs and bars here (which simply means the dancers perform naked). Years ago, someone from another church called me to suggest that we get our congregations to picket these clubs. Well, what good would that do, other than simply advertise these places, getting them time on local television news? Instead, our women's ministries prayerfully searched for ways of impacting those clubs (note I said our *women's* ministries). As a result, they began invading those night spots, bringing gifts and love to the dancers rather than condemnation. Currently, over 125 of those dancers have accepted Christ as Savior, have left the clubs, and we have assisted them in getting jobs and homes. The first of those converts led our bus ministry for several years before moving to another city. This is another example of practicing a godly worldview of the lost. Week after week, I see those ladies scattered throughout the congregation, singing the songs of the redeemed and praising the Lord.

Another fascinating outreach ministry is our God-mobile. One of our board members and his wife take the God-mobile to various fairs around southwest Florida, park it on the midway, and talk to people about their souls. This year alone, 351 people have prayed to ask Christ into their lives. These new believers then receive a basic new believer's course that's available in several languages. We are presently negotiating to add a second God-mobile to reach even more people for Christ.

Let's discuss the cost of a godly worldview. Isn't it expensive? I suspect that depends upon your estimate of the value of one eternal soul. The late evangelist Jack Shuler, who led me to Christ in 1950, wrote:

> The human soul, of all God's vast creation, alone is priceless. All earth's fabulous billions are not enough to buy a soul. Place on the counter the cities with their skyscrapers, hotels and factories, and the sum would be inadequate. Add the continents with their precious minerals and vast resources, and still the amount would be insufficient. The earth with its mountains, plains and seas, its gold silver and

oil, its diamonds and pearls—even the staggering wealth of these could not purchase one immortal soul. The soul is eternal![8]

Money can never be the deciding factor in reaching the lost. Yes, reaching the lost can be expensive, but God has promised to provide every need. When Jesus commissioned His followers to go into all the world and preach the gospel to every creature (Mark 16:15), He promised that signs and wonders would follow those who believed. That promise could refer to the new believers, of course; but it also applies to those obedient to the divine commission. Resources always follow obedience. Rarely are the resources there ahead of time.

It should be clear to the reader by this time how urgent the call to missions is in our church. We have a missionary speak every Wednesday night and at least once a quarter in our weekend services. We also bring in another half dozen missionaries or so from around the world in our November missions convention. The Wednesday night offering goes to the missionary—every cent of it. I always give a strong plea to our people to give as God lays it on their hearts. That's no small goal, I assure you! Our church survives on the weekend offerings. As already described in this book, in our missions convention we receive faith promises for the coming year. In 1987 that figure was a little over $220,000. This year it will exceed $3 million. So how do we function? How do we survive financially?

We are not "buildings" driven. Most of our buildings are decades old. We're careful how we spend God's money. Still, this church can't do what it does based on its size. The only rationale is God's supernatural power. For example, as I write this we are preparing for this year's missions convention. We are bringing in missionaries from Israel, Jordan, and Romania. The whole week will cost a ton of money. Last week I asked the Lord to help us. After all, the purpose of the convention is to obey His commission. Out of absolutely nowhere came a check that covered the entire need. Incredible, to be sure, but I have seen this happen again and again. Signs and wonders do follow those who believe.

Church leadership that embraces a godly worldview must exhibit strong faith. Why? Because the commission Christ has given us can't be done in our own power or resources. It is impossible. But God never gives us a direction without a resource. If church leadership waits for the resource to come first, the church will never see much done for the kingdom.

Ask yourself, Does the church I attend have a godly worldview? Can we see God's provision? Do we really encompass our city, our area, and our world (Jerusalem, Judea, Samaria, and the uttermost part of the earth) in the way that pleases the One who died for it? If not, why not? And what will you do about it?

CHAPTER  EIGHTEEN

AFTERWORD

As I WRITE THIS FINAL CHAPTER, OUR CHURCH IS IN THE MIDDLE OF OUR ANNUAL MISSIONS CONVENTION WEEK —"THE MOTOR OF OUR CHURCH." Yesterday I listened to a missionary from Bucharest, Romania, and my heart felt like it was melting in my chest. I hasten to add that in all my world travels, Bucharest is probably my least favorite city. I was there not long after the fall of Nicolae Ceausescu, the brutal communist tyrant who ruled Romania for twenty-one years. It was a brutally-cold winter, snow stacked everywhere, and winds howling through the frozen streets. About the only place a homeless person could get warm was in the underground system of massive heat pipes that brought some semblance of heat to the city's buildings. In those "sewers" thousands of people were trying to stay alive. Children, dying from hunger and frostbite, meandered through the streets, rags soaked with glue over their faces. The fumes from the glue seemed to deaden the pain of these doomed children while at the same time eating away their brains. Communism breeds hopelessness, especially since the people have been indoctrinated that there is no God.

All those long years ago I met a young man who had recently found Jesus Christ as his Savior. His girlfriend, now his wife of twenty years, had become a follower of Jesus and led him to salvation. He was anxious to do something for the Lord. Today he serves as the director of Teen Challenge in Romania. As he spoke, he began listing the missions accomplishments of our church through the years in that beleaguered land. I had almost forgotten how our little group cleaned and repainted a burn unit in Bucharest during that initial trip. There we saw children, some with second and third degree burns, dying in that filthy hovel called a "hospital." Our missionary related to us that some of those kids survived, partly through our efforts, and were now adults and living strong godly lives. Oh, the joy that filled my mind and heart as I heard those stories.

Then the Holy Spirit brought to my mind passages from the Word that tell of a day when we will see firsthand the results of our missions efforts, not only in Romania but in so many parts of the world:

> After these things I looked, and behold, a great multitude which no one could number, of all nations, tribes, peoples, and tongues, standing before the throne and before the Lamb, clothed with white robes, with palm branches in their hands, and crying out with a loud voice, saying, "Salvation belongs to our God who sits on the throne, and to the Lamb!" All the angels stood around the throne and the elders and the four living creatures, and fell on their faces before the throne and worshiped God, saying: "Amen! Blessing and glory and wisdom, thanksgiving and honor and power and might, be to our God forever and ever. Amen." (Rev. 7:9–12)

While that passage is usually interpreted as having to do with people saved during the tribulation, it also reveals to us the numerical magnitude of saints around God's throne. I once heard a pastor tell his missions-minded congregation that after just a couple minutes in heaven, as multitudes of people flocked around them to express gratitude for the part those people had played in their salvation, they would rejoice for every dollar they had ever invested in missions. What a worthy investment! Houses come and go. Hulks of once-expensive automobiles rust in junk yards. The best of clothes go out of style. But what we have invested in souls for Christ lasts forever.

I remember we used to sing the little chorus: With eternity's values in view, Lord, with eternity's values in view / May I do each day's work for you, Lord, with eternity's values in view!

The passage in Revelation 7 informs us that the saved around the throne will be a vast crowd, truly beyond all human calculating. The redeemed will come from every tribe and nation. This is why Jesus commanded us to go into *all the world* to preach the gospel, not just our own town. There we will see the joyful hosts clad in the very righteousness of Christ Himself, singing praises to God's precious Lamb.

I feel good because I'm investing my life and funds into the eternal destiny of lost souls for whom my beloved Savior gave His life.

From every pulpit should go forth proclamations of eternal truths. Too often we hear shallow messages teaching "feel-good-ism" religion. Yes, my faith makes me feel wonderful, but why? Because I'm getting a nice car, another room on my house, or a better suit of clothes? No! I feel good because I'm investing my life and funds into the eternal destiny of lost souls for whom my beloved Savior gave His life.

For over fifty years, it has been my joy to be a servant of the King. He has allowed me the exquisite privilege of being a pastor of a local church. I could ask for no higher reason to live. God has blessed me by inserting into my life giants of the faith who have injected me with the reality of eternity. How powerfully they taught me that this old world is not my home. I truly am just passing through. I know that my own personal journey is nearing its conclusion sooner, rather than later. And my heart is filled with joy. I'm anxious to see my brother and other family members who have made the leap from earth to Glory. I'm overwhelmed at the prospect of seeing my Lord, face-to-face. I'm also joyous with the reality of seeing those multitudes of whom John wrote, people our church has reached with the gospel. I will rejoice for every missionary who ever graced our church platform. I will bless every single day of decades of annual missionary conventions. I will lift my hands in praise for every faith promise for missions given.

Do you think when that time comes that I will think back on the architecture of our church buildings? The cleverness of our church stationery? The type of music we employed in our services? I doubt if any of those peripheral issues will ever even come to mind.

Churches that are blessed, now and for eternity, are those that understand Jesus' Great Commission, and who follow it faithfully and relentlessly. God will never inquire of us how nice our church buildings were. He will never ask about the uniqueness of our sermon outlines. The subject of our election to positions will never come up. What He will inquire of us is, "Were you faithful to my Son's commandment to take the whole gospel to the whole world?"

And behold, I am coming quickly; and My reward is with Me, to give every one according to his work. (Rev. 22:12)

What a promise! What a warning! What a challenge! May your church be blessed!

 **ENDNOTES**

1. *All the Nations* by Chris Davis, http://www.higherpraise.com/lyrics/awesome/awesome6530.html
2. http://en.wikipedia.org/wiki/Oswald_J._Smith
3. *Is That All There Is*, 1969, Jerry Lieber and Mike Stoller.
4. Oswald J. Smith, *The Challenge of Missions* (New York: Harper-Collins Publishing, 1980), 62–63.
5. John H. Sammis, 1887, http://library.timelesstruths.org/music/Trust_and_Obey/
6. George Barna, *The Power of Vision* (Grand Rapids, MI: Baker Books, 2009), 9.
7. https://www.barna.org/barna-update/culture/698-10-facts-about-america-s-churchless
8. Jack Shuler, *Shuler's Short Sermons* (Grand Rapids, MI: Zondervan, 1951), 18–19.

✿ ABOUT THE AUTHOR

Dan Betzer is the senior pastor of First Assembly of God in Fort Myers, Florida, where he has pastored for the past twenty-nine years. During those years, he has seen the congregation grow from a few hundred to its current 10,000 members and adherents with an average weekend attendance of 6,700 including the satellite campuses.

Ordained fifty-two years ago, Dan is a lifelong veteran of broadcasting and is known as a writer, television and radio host, and district and national executive with the General Council of the Assemblies of God. At the age of three, Betzer began radio work on WNAX in Sioux City, Iowa, doing children's and religious programs each weekend, singing and acting. By the time he was in college, he was a daily anchor on both radio and television news. Profoundly sensing God's direction, he entered the ministry and began planting churches in Ohio.

Betzer served as the assistant district superintendent of the Peninsular Florida District of the Assemblies of God for sixteen years and carried the portfolio of World Missions. He is now an honorary presbyter in that district.

For the past twenty years he has served as an executive presbyter of the General Council of the Assemblies of God, which is the twenty-member general board of directors of the denomination. He has been a part of the general presbytery for twenty-two years.

For nearly seventeen years (1979–1995), Betzer was the speaker on the Assemblies of God syndicated radio broadcast *Revivaltime*, which was heard on over 600 stations each week in over 80 countries. He also wrote and hosted the two-minute weekday radio program *Byline*, heard on several hundred stations, and also wrote and hosted the one-minute television version, seen on scores of stations worldwide each weekday (TBN, CTN, Family-Net, Cornerstone Network, and Daystar). He currently hosts nine television programs and one radio program each week in southwest Florida.

As a soloist, Dan has produced seventeen albums and has sung with artists such as Ralph Carmichael and his orchestra, Dino, Larry Gatlin, the Blackwood Brothers, Lulu Roman, The Couriers, and many others. Betzer has authored twenty-one published books, including a best-selling novel.

Betzer has been married to his wife, Darlene, for fifty-nine years. They have three daughters, one son, eight grandchildren, and four great-grandchildren. For relaxation, Dan enjoys traveling (he has ministered in sixty-two nations), playing golf, fishing, and reading.

For More Information

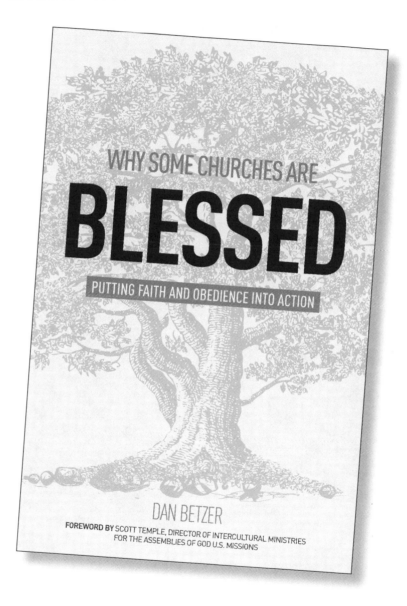

WHY SOME CHURCHES ARE

BLESSED

PUTTING FAITH AND OBEDIENCE INTO ACTION

DAN BETZER

FOREWORD BY SCOTT TEMPLE, DIRECTOR OF INTERCULTURAL MINISTRIES
FOR THE ASSEMBLIES OF GOD U.S. MISSIONS

For more information about this and other valuable resources
visit www.gospelpublishing.com